Antonio Carluccio
An Invitation to Italian Cooking

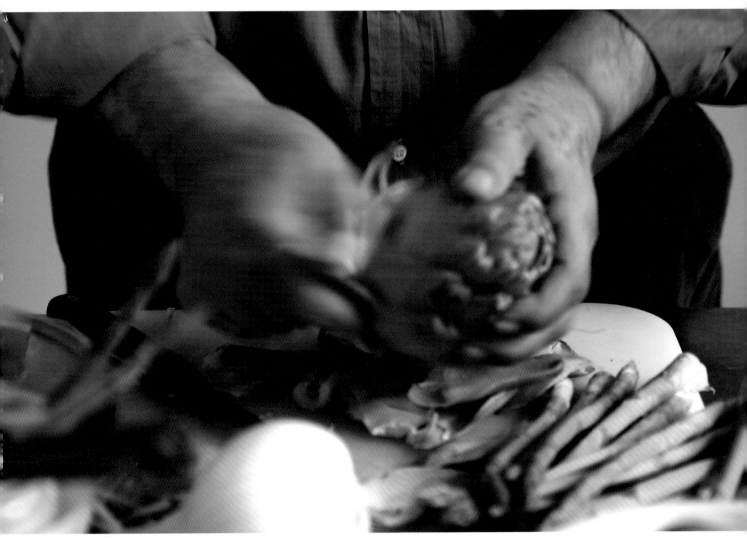

Photographs by Steve Lee

Illustrations by Flo Bayley

headline

Dedication

With profound
gratitude to everyone
who assisted in
the rebirth of
*An Invitation to
Italian Cooking*

Acknowledgements

I would like to thank
the following people:
Susan Fleming
Giselle Blake-Davies
Heather Holden-Brown
Lorraine Jerram
Bryone Picton
Pat White
Alastair Hendy
Steve Lee
Becca Hetherston
Flo Bayley
Priscilla Carluccio

Copyright © 2002 Antonio Carluccio

The right of Antonio Carluccio to be identified as the
Author of the Work has been asserted by him in accordance
with the Copyright, Designs and Patents Act 1988.

Photographs © 2002 Steve Lee
Illustrations © 2002 Flo Bayley

First published in 2002 by
HEADLINE BOOK PUBLISHING

10 9 8 7 6 5 4 3 2 1

Cataloguing in Publication Data available from the British Library

ISBN 0 7472 7590 4

Edited by Susan Fleming
Designed by Andrew Barron @ Thextension
Photography by Steve Lee
Home economy by Becca Hetherston
Food styling and photographic art direction by Alastair Hendy
Map by ML Design

Reproduction by Spectrum Colour, Suffolk, UK
Printed and bound in France by Imprimerie Pollina s.a.

HEADLINE BOOK PUBLISHING
A division of Hodder Headline
338 Euston Road, London NW1 3BH
www.headline.co.uk
www.hodderheadline.com

contents

introduction

I have been passionate about food and cooking all of my life. As a child, I used to spend hours in the kitchen watching my mother cooking, and I found it fascinating. But it wasn't until I was around twenty, that I discovered the excitement and exhilaration of cooking for myself.

The food I ate during my childhood was very good indeed. Even in wartime when there were severe food shortages, we were extraordinarily lucky. My father was station-master in Castelnuovo Belbo, a little town near Alessandria in the north of Italy. On one occasion the Germans destroyed two bridges, one on either side of the village, while a goods train was pulled up at the station. It was full of provisions such as rice and oil, which we shared with the villagers and exchanged for fresh bread and salami and cheese.

Later, we moved to Borgofranco d'Ivrea, situated in the Aosta valley, north of Turin. My happiest memories of those schooldays were the lunches. I went to school in Ivrea, which is about seven kilometres from Borgofranco. Since it was too far to go home in the middle of the day, my mother used to send my lunch via a goods train. Every day I would wait in the Ivrea station, impatient for the moment when the guard handed me that wonderful little basket. Inside there would be a complete meal – hot soup, a little meat or fish with vegetables, some cheese, bread, and a piece of fruit. The menu changed every day! In summer I used to eat it sitting on a pile of sleepers, completely alone. I could really concentrate on my lunch, it was so peaceful. When you grow up with pleasant experiences like that, you can't help but love food.

I started cooking after I moved to Vienna as a student, to continue my language studies. I used to telephone my mother to ask how to cook particular dishes. A few years later, when I went to Germany to start my career in the wine trade, I found myself doing more and more cooking, mostly for friends. I came to England in 1975, to set up as a wine merchant, and my professional, gastronomic career took off five years later when I was runner-up in an amateur best cook competition run by the *Sunday Times* magazine.

An Invitation to Italian Cooking was written a few years later, almost ten years into my English experience. In the fifteen or so years since then, I have seen a huge change in the awareness of Italian food by the British. That first publication of my *Invitation* might have had something to do with it, but for me, more importantly, it was the first expression of what Italian food actually meant to me. In researching that book (which has been followed by many others), I learned to appreciate what I had grown up with, the northern cooking of my childhood, and to recognise the truly regional nature of Italian food, something that is very much reflected here. This 'new *Invitation*' has been largely rewritten, but preserving those aspects of Italian food that will never change, while introducing fresh ideas and ingredients that have become familiar and more widely available in the intervening years.

In fact Italian food has been enjoying a huge renaissance all over the world, with everyone coming to realise how delicious it is, relying as it does so heavily on local, seasonal and the very freshest of ingredients, and also how easy the recipes are to cook. The simplest way of describing what characterises Italian cookery is that it involves the minimum of fuss, and the maximum of flavour.

I hope that you will enjoy my new *Invitation*. Buon appetito!

Carluccio

italian meals

One thing that becomes obvious if you travel around Italy is the enormous variety of local dishes. The food is distinctly regional in character and the raw ingredients, mostly locally grown or raised, are chosen with great care. Quality and freshness are supremely important.

All Italians have been brought up to be knowledgeable about food. They can recognise good food and, even if they don't cook themselves, they know exactly how it should taste. This education starts at a very early age. If children – particularly boys who tend to be a bit spoiled – don't like the food they are given, they will be offered something else. And I remember that, like most Italian men, my father was very critical. The first thing he would say when he came to the table was, 'It needs more salt', or 'It's overcooked'. Compliments were given sparingly. So I knew that food should be treated very seriously indeed. And I learned later, when I started to cook myself, just how valuable compliments are (and how dispiriting criticism is)!

There is no doubt Italians live for food. They think and talk about it constantly, and they spend a lot of money on it (especially at lunch time). Of course this obsession with food is a very old one. The ancient Romans were famous for their gastronomic excesses. The Florentines and Venetians of Renaissance Italy held sumptuous banquets that were talked about the length and breadth of Europe. They were the gourmets of the western world. Even the French learned many of the basics from the Italians. When Catherine de' Medici went to France to marry the future Henri II she took fifty cooks with her. They introduced cooking techniques and foods which were unknown in France – béchamel sauce, for instance, petits pois and artichokes among them.

Unlike the French chefs, the Italians never forgot the age-old principles of their cooking – it is always simple and straightforward, never overloaded with fancy sauces, and only the best, seasonal ingredients are used. It is that approach which is found in the French provinces surrounding the Mediterranean, especially Provence (parts of it belonged to the Italian House of Savoy until well into the nineteenth century). In Provence you will eat dishes that have a strong Italian influence: anchoïade, pistou, pissaladière (a version of pizza), and the lightly cooked vegetables sautéed in olive oil and garlic, for instance.

And unlike the French, the Italians only flirted for a brief time with 'nouvelle cuisine' . They got tired of eating minimal portions of pretty food, and soon returned to traditional regional cooking, very often creating a new trend with the rediscovery of wonderful peasant dishes. However, nouvelle cuisine did leave some good influences: the more appropriate use of fats, for instance, and a new interest in the presentation of dishes.

Breakfast For most Italians in the towns and cities, breakfast is just an espresso. Anyone who is hungry will have a 'panino' (a bread roll with a savoury filling) at a café. Or they will eat brioche or little cakes – but usually nothing too salty. Children have hot sweetened milk and coffee into which they dip bread or biscuits. When I was young I remember the best time for breakfast was around Christmas. My father used to be given panettone (Christmas cake) as presents from companies, and there were always so many they would last until the middle of January. We would have a delicious slice with hot milk every morning.

The evening meal This, like breakfast, is a fairly minor event. It is usually quite light, perhaps a little brodino (light soup) or an omelette, and it is often eaten quite late, particularly in the south. There, when it is very hot, the people go out in the evening and meet their friends on the corso and have an espresso or an aperitif. They go home and eat about ten or eleven o'clock, just before going to bed. In the big industrial centres, some workers will have a three- or four-course meal at night if they haven't had the time to go home in the middle of the day.

Lunch Traditionally lunch is the most important meal of the day. The first-time visitor to Italy is usually a little bewildered by the way everything stops in the middle of the day for two or three hours. The shops close, churches are locked, the museums are shut, streets empty and the only visible activity is in the restaurants and the cafés. This is the point, when the sun is at its zenith, that Italians focus all their attention on the glories of the table. Now, although that is changing in the big towns, most families still come home and eat their midday meal together. It is a leisurely, communal affair, with plenty of time to concentrate on the food and on the conversation.

Sometimes it will start with an antipasto – perhaps a few slices of salami, or some roasted peppers. Just a little thing. And then always a first course (il primo): a pasta or a soup, or maybe risotto. After that there will be a small portion of meat or fish (il secondo), accompanied by either lightly cooked vegetables or a salad. Cheese, which is always eaten with bread, and fruit are served at the end, followed by an espresso. Local wine and mineral water will be drunk, and throughout the meal great quantities of bread will be consumed.

The structure of an Italian meal The lunch-time meal described above demonstrates the true artistry of Italian cooking. It is planned so that each course is in harmony with all the others: the tastes, the textures, the richness and the quantities are all perfectly balanced. A slightly heavy antipasto, such as vitello tonnato or eggs with truffles, would be followed by a primo or first course such as a light soup, perhaps just a consommé. After a very light antipasto like bresaola della Valtellina or a mixture of pickles with salami, you would have a primo of pasta or risotto. A delicately flavoured food, such as asparagus risotto, is never preceded by something that will overwhelm it – carciofi sott'olio or porcini sott'olio would be ideal. And you would never serve two very rich foods at the same meal: you wouldn't follow a fish soup with venison, for example.

There are so many perfect combinations it is hard to choose just one. But if I were cooking a very special meal, I might base it all on fish. I would offer baked stuffed anchovies as an antipasto, followed by fettuccine nere – a pasta flavoured and coloured with cuttlefish ink – as a primo. Then a simple fish dish would be appropriate as a secondo or main course, something like fritto misto di pesce, accompanied by lemon wedges and a simple salad (i vegetali). I would serve a little piece of stracchino for the cheese course, and fragole all'aceto balsamico (strawberries with balsamic vinegar) to finish. And I would choose Gavi dei Gavi, a very dry white wine, to drink throughout the meal.

Within all the formality described above, there is a feeling of immediacy and of sheer passion for food. There is continuous variety, keeping the diner's appetite and imagination constantly stimulated.

ingredients

If I had to choose a few basic ingredients to take with me to a desert island to conjure up the flavours of Italian cooking, I wouldn't hesitate to plump for olive oil, tomatoes, hard-grain flour, Parmesan cheese, plus some garlic and basil. Without these basics, Italian cooking would lose its essential character and become unrecognisable. Of course, there would need to be eggs to make the pasta, and yeast for pizza dough, and pepper, and nutmeg; and a grater for the Parmesan, and my favourite knife, and perhaps a pasta machine… Maybe I could grow my own tomatoes and herbs, and settle instead for a supply of Parma ham, and certainly plenty of fresh ricotta. Perhaps the island would have woods where I'd be able to find my favourite wild mushrooms, and doubtless there'd be plenty of first-class seafood. Then again, I would miss polenta, risotto rice, and pecorino cheese… And what about wine?

The best and only solution would be to try and choose a desert island with a superb Italian delicatessen!

The desert island fantasy, in a sense, represents the challenge of cooking the Italian way in any country other than Italy – something that is much more achievable now, fifteen or so years after the first publication of *An Invitation to Italian Cooking*. It's a question of choosing top-quality fresh ingredients, combining them with certain essential items from the store-cupboard, and then preparing and cooking them in characteristic ways. By taking a look at Italian shopping tactics for fresh ingredients, seeing what's in the store-cupboard, and surveying the equipment in an Italian kitchen (see page 18), I hope that the following pages will provide a useful background for the actual recipes in the rest of the book.

A few years ago I was invited to India to teach Italian cooking to fifteen executive chefs working for a national chain of luxury hotels, and I was to use locally available ingredients as far as I could to avoid the complications of importing them. I was able to find 80 per cent of what I needed from local produce, but the rest, like Parmesan, dried porcini, olive oil, salami, Parma ham, pancetta and flours, had to be sent for from elsewhere in the country.

Now, however, Italian food is so popular all over the world that basic ingredients are available almost everywhere. The supermarkets are importing the ingredients people demand after they have seen them on television and read about them in the many thousands of cookery books published every year. But there is a growing number of independent delicatessens beginning to import that very special range of artisanal food which allows authentic Italian food to be prepared. In 1991 I started to import some very specially selected items, and we not only sell them in my Carluccio's delicatessen next to the Neal Street Restaurant, but we distribute wholesale to more than a hundred independent delicatessens worldwide. In fact, a few years ago, we decided to expand, and have opened a series of shops which are caffè, delicatessen and restaurant rolled into one.

Every year, my wife and I are importing new items, wanting to provoke and encourage a new interest in flavours and culinary sensations. It is a form of education, we feel, and the success we have enjoyed proves that Italian food has many lovers and many converts. Shopping for good ingredients is one of the most important aspects of producing a good meal, and the information in the next few pages should be part of that learning process.

As a little boy I was almost always sent to do the shopping. My mother would give me the shopping list and inspect everything I brought back very carefully. So I learned the art of choosing immediately and well.

Many a time I have fallen into the trap of dutifully making out a shopping list and then finding that none of the ingredients I want is available. The lesson gradually sank in. Now when I am planning a meal I always leave the choice open in case I have to rethink the whole of the menu, buying what looks like good quality in terms of freshness, appearance and price when I am actually at the market.

The ability to know at first sight whether meat is tender, or peaches are fresh yet ripe, comes from long experience, but is an insight that can easily be developed by someone who is really interested in obtaining excellent results. It is always best to scout around first in order to find the best produce on offer and to compare prices. Although in many instances you may irritate the seller by seeming to be fussy, by knowing exactly what you want you may also gain his respect.

Meat

You need to find a trustworthy butcher, who understands you and gives you exactly what you require. An understanding butcher is one who will sell you the cut of meat most suitable for the dish you intend to prepare, so don't hesitate to tell him what it is you are planning.

Beef Good beef should be bright red, with the grain neither too swollen nor tight. The fat should be pale yellow, which shows that the beef has been hung for some days after butchering. This releases the muscles and tenderises the meat.

Veal Veal meat is obtained from calves butchered when they are only ten weeks old and still feeding from their mothers (milk-fed). The meat should be pale pink. In Italy we can get an older veal meat, called 'vitellone', which is a darker pink.

Lamb In Italy the best lamb comes from Tuscany, the Abruzzo and the south. The animal should be less than a year old when it is butchered, otherwise the meat acquires an intense taste like mutton. In fact, as with veal, milk-fed lambs are available in some areas. The colour of good lamb is dark pink, and it should be firm to the touch.

Pork Pork meat should be pale and firm. If you are buying either 'salumi' or 'insaccati misti' (meaning literally 'bagged pieces' like salami, sausages etc.), be sure to ascertain from the label that the amount of pork meat is greater than the fat, at least 60–70 per cent.

Poultry and Game

It is vital to consider the origins of the bird, and what food it has been fed on, as well as choosing the type that suits your purpose. Trust your butcher or poulterer to buy well.

Chickens and cockerels The best are free-range, not battery-bred, and fed on polenta (Italy) or corn (elsewhere). They are usually quite old, containing a considerable quantity of fat, and are suitable for making broths and stocks.

Roasting chicken These should not exceed 1.5kg (3 lb) in weight. The meat must be tender, but not soft, and a little fat adds the required juiciness.

Poussin This is a young bird usually about eight to nine weeks old. It should weigh around 400g (14 oz). It is usually marinated first, then grilled for maximum tenderness.

Turkey Those sold in Britain or in America can weigh up to 15–18kg (30–33 lb), but in Italy you will never find a bird of more than 10kg (22 lb). The meat of a young and tender turkey is pale; if it is old, the meat will be considerably more stringy and tough.

Ducks and geese Neither of these should be too young, as the meat will not have developed good enough flavour, but neither should they be too old, when the meat becomes very fatty and tends to be leathery. Duck is usually to be found the whole year round, whereas goose is more a winter (and specifically Christmas) fowl. Wild duck is slightly smaller than the domestic breeds, and the meat is darker in colour and more intense in taste. Goose naturally contains more fat, and may weigh anything up to 4kg (9 lb).

Wild fowl Wild birds include quail and guinea fowl (although both are now bred for the table), pheasants, pigeon, woodcock and partridge, as well, I'm afraid, as the thrush and sparrow. Italians are still much derided for their passion for the hunting and consumption of such small wild birds. I prefer to see them freely flying in the countryside, but I have to confess that I have eaten them…

Hare and rabbit Both these creatures are popular in Italian cooking, particularly in Tuscany, and rabbit is now bred for the table. The meat of both animals is tender and white, and often it is only the size of the bones that will allow you to tell one from the other. When choosing rabbit, be careful about its age: it should not be more than six or seven months old. The neck should be quite short and the legs long. Wild rabbit is smaller than the bred variety.

Fish

When you are shopping for fish, the most important quality to look for is, naturally, freshness. The eyes should be clear, transparent and without a red glazing; the gills should be a bright red and the scales shiny and slimy in texture. The final test, of course, is the fresh smell of the fish.

A trustworthy fishmonger's fish and shellfish will be surrounded by ice to keep them as fresh as possible. He will be selling shellfish that come from non-contaminated waters: particularly important when you want things like oysters or mussels, which are either eaten raw or very lightly cooked.

Nowadays frozen fish is becoming the norm in cities and inland towns (where once they relied on salted or dried fish). This convenient alternative to fresh fish can produce good results, but only if your supplier is really trustworthy. Indeed, to be really good, the fish should have been frozen immediately after being caught. A newer development in the fish industry is fish farming, and, although some purists claim to be able to tell the difference, farmed salmon, sea bass and sea bream etc. are a valuable addition to our shopping lists.

Vegetables and Fruit

When shopping for vegetables and fruit, it is always a good idea to scout around first in order to see which is the best produce and to see what is newly in season. One of the pleasantest fruit and vegetable markets that I know takes place at Porta Palazzo in Turin. Here you can find an astounding variety of northern specialities as well as other wonderful vegetables introduced by southerners, especially those from Puglia, Sicily and Calabria. Owing to the influx of immigrants bringing with them from the south the basic ingredients of their home cooking, the people of northern Italy have become accustomed to using vegetables that did not appear in traditional Piedmontese gastronomy. The same adaptability is, of course, being displayed by the immigrants, in their use of local northern ingredients. A similar development has become increasingly noticeable in other large cosmopolitan communities, especially London, New York and Paris. In my view, the greater the choice of ingredients available the more exciting and interesting the preparation of any meal becomes.

Always try to buy vegetables and fruit that are currently in season rather than imported produce which could probably be both more expensive and less tasty since it is either grown in a greenhouse or picked immature and allowed to ripen in crates on the journey.

Groceries

It is usually best to put yourself in the hands of a good Italian delicatessen. Groceries that you should never be without include: olive oil, risotto rice, good dried pasta, dried mushrooms, canned tomatoes, anchovies (preferably salted), capers (again preferably salted), dried and possibly canned beans (beans and tomatoes are the only acceptable canned goods in my Italian kitchen), polenta and hard-grain or plain flours, salt, pepper and garlic.

Olive Oil

Although it is one of the fundamental ingredients of Italian cooking, by no means all Italians use olive oil extensively in their cooking. Indeed, butter is more commonly used in northern Italy. However, all Italians do eat salads and certain other specialities dressed with olive oil, and for these recipes the real thing is indispensable. A huge range of olive oils is now available from delicatessens, supermarkets, even by mail order, so never settle for anything less.

Olive oils are now classified in a way that is similar to the DOC classification of many wines.

Extra virgin olive oil This is the result of the first, cold pressing of the olives, and is very green in colour, slightly opaque, and viscous rather than fluid. It has a very pungent taste – differing from region to region – and the full quality of its flavour and texture is best appreciated raw, which is why it is recommended for salads and uncooked sauces, as well as for *Fresella, Pinzimonio* (see pages 182 and 180), bruschetta, and for drizzling on top of soups etc. The best extra virgin olive oils are still quite expensive to buy, but worth every drop.

Virgin olive oil This is less green and more yellowish in colour, is runnier and can be used more generously. It is ideal for salads, mayonnaise and for general cooking purposes, such as frying when the olive oil taste is required.

'Pure' olive oil Successive heated pressings of the olives produce oils which are more or less refined and blended, and can be used in all types of cooking. If the oil is of good quality, the flavour will still be distinctive, but bland enough to be used in frying and general cooking.

Whenever 'oil' is mentioned in the ingredients of a recipe, use olive oil (the recipes specify which quality).

Cereals and Grains

Rice Arborio, carnaroli and vialone rices are indispensable for risottos, and are grown mostly on the Pianura Padana on the plain of the Po between the provinces of Vercelli, Novara, Milan and Verona. The main characteristic that makes these rices ideal for risottos is the fatness and starchiness of the grain which enables it to swell to at least three times its original volume, while still retaining a firm al dente texture.

Flour With their pastas, pizzas and breads, the Italians use a lot of flour, and in fact most of their meals are accompanied by something starchy. The wheat grown in southern Italy, particularly Apulia, and on the plains of North America and Russia, is durum wheat, a hard-grained variety which when milled has a slightly granular texture as opposed to the softer powdery flour commonly used for bread-making and other cooking. It also contains more gluten than other wheats. Commercially made pasta must, in Italy, be made from 'pura semola di grano duro'; you can check this on the label. Pasta made from this flour stands up to cooking very well, swells in cooking to increase its volume by over 20 per cent, and is also both nutritious and easily digestible. For making home-made pasta and gnocchi, you may be able to find this semolina flour (not to be confused with the semolina used in puddings) in any Italian delicatessen, and increasingly in good supermarkets.

On the other hand, plain flour, preferably unbleached, makes perfectly good home-made pasta all'uovo, if you follow the recipe proportions and quantities accurately and work the dough to the right texture. (In the absence of gluten, the egg proteins give the cooked pasta its al dente texture.) It is also perfect for pizza doughs. It needs no extra sifting. The Italian equivalent of this is called '00' or 'doppio zero', and this is now widely available.

Dried pasta My belief is that fresh pasta is always better than dried, but it depends, of course, on where you get it! Italians mostly use dried commercial pasta of good quality every day, and then enjoy home-made egg pasta at weekends. (On special occasions, neighbours or friends come and help with making large quantities of ravioli or tortellini, or special hand-shaped pastas such as fusilli and orecchiette.)

There are certain 'rules' about eating and serving pasta. There are over 600 different shapes of pasta, all of which have been created to accompany, enhance and complement endless sauces. For example, you must never eat large-shaped pasta with seafood sauces, but only thin strings such as linguine, spaghettini or tagliatellini. And stuffed pastas only need simple sauces, such as melted butter or a light tomato sauce.

Polenta Originally from Mexico, maize gradually, throughout the last four centuries, assumed the role of a major starch in Italy, in the north particularly. Maize, much the same as sweetcorn, was and is still fed to animals, but it is even more fascinating that something which was such a staple should now be a speciality, cooked in many ways to satisfy a desire for more complex flavours and textures. Once polenta became the subject of food fashion abroad, like many other ingredients, everyone wanted to taste it, and many first reactions were that it was boring, just like porridge. But the inhabitants of the northern Alpine valleys added cheese and butter, which makes the polenta truly exquisite.

The coarsely ground corn meal is cooked with water and salt in a traditional copper pan, usually fired by wood. In this way polenta, stirred for 40 or so minutes, became stiffer and this is the point when it is either eaten hot and wet, or cooled down and set after which it is sliced to be grilled or fried.

There is now a new kind of polenta, which is precooked, and is ready in only 5 minutes. You have to stir it a lot. There is also a white polenta from a white variety of maize. This is used in the Veneto and in the south of Italy.

Bread The Italians eat a great deal of bread, and almost every region has its local specialities, using local ingredients. They don't go to the lengths of the French, however, baking it twice a day. Most Italian bread is still good in the evening, and in some cases, even better the next day! In the Aosta valley and other Alpine valleys, for instance, the inhabitants bake only once a month, as the bread is a longer-lasting variety, made of dark barley flour. It is only edible when reconstituted in water. Alternatively, in the south you will find bread in long shapes which is baked weekly. This bread is usually made to be sliced and then toasted as bruschetta, or to break up and use as a binder in soups. They use hard durum wheat mixed with tender wheat flour, and the bread, mostly baked in wood-fired ovens, smells and tastes fabulous. The most famous is that of Altamura in Puglia.

An exception is the bread made in Sardinia. The 'pane carasau' is a very thin bread which is double baked and cut in half to obtain two discs 30cm (12 in) in diameter which are completely dry. It can be kept for a long time, and can be brought back to life by sprinkling it with water to be used in a salad or a soup.

Tuscany produces a bread which is made without salt, called 'pane sciocco', or 'silly bread'. In Piedmont they are very fond of small rolls, 'panini all'olio', which are made with olive oil or butter to obtain a greater crumbliness. Perhaps the most typical of that region, now familiar well beyond the shores of Italy, are the dry and crunchy grissini, sticks of baked bread dough eaten with the antipasti.

Other popular breads which have taken over in the rest of Europe are focaccia and ciabatta. The first looks like a thick pizza, but has the texture of bread, and is made in various ways throughout Italy, most usually with lots of olive oil, but often topped with other ingredients. The ciabatta is more modern, and is named for the down-at-heel slipper or loafer its shape resembles.

Breadcrumbs Every bread shop in Italy sells good breadcrumbs, fresh and dry; they make their own. Dry crumbs for coating are easy to make by toasting bread in the oven and then putting the golden pieces of bread through a food processor. The same, of course, applies to making fresh at home: use good, preferably day-old bread, cut off the crusts, and blitz in the processor.

Tomatoes

The Italian 'pomodoro', meaning 'golden apple', reflects the almost mythical veneration attached to this versatile fruit. When I first moved away from Italy, it was difficult to find satisfactory quantities of fresh tomatoes. I soon overcame my prejudice against the canned variety (for sauces, at least), however, provided that these are of good quality. Not all canned tomatoes are good. Look for deep red fruit, preferably of the 'fiaschetta' variety, which is plum shaped, meaty and has relatively few seeds. The surrounding liquid should be thick and not too watery. Ask for 'San Marzano' peeled tomatoes, named after the town in the province of Salerno where enormous quantities of tomatoes are grown exclusively for canning. Canned tomatoes are available already chopped up for use in sauces, but it is easy enough to chop them in the can with a long knife or long kitchen scissors.

Also available now is passata di pomodoro, which is a very finely strained tomato sauce. This is too much like a juice to be useful to me, although it might have its place in soups. Much more labour-saving is polpa di pomodoro, which includes chunks of tomatoes, and can often be used in place of canned tomatoes.

Fresh tomatoes for sauces should always be fully ripened, whether they are round, beefsteak, plum or some of the mini varieties such as cherry. Canned ones are preferable to unripe fresh ones. Skin tomatoes if needed by immersing them in boiling water for a minute, then peeling the skin off. De-seed if necessary. In the markets of southern Italy you can find a type of small round tomato with a tough skin; they are very sweet, meaty and juicy inside, and are good for sauces.

For salads, the Italians prefer beefsteak tomatoes, and they delight in eating these meaty tomatoes almost green.

Sun-dried tomatoes are now available, with or without olive oil, and the ones in oil make an excellent antipasto. I have given a recipe for 'sun-drying' your own tomatoes at home

(see page 33). There are also now tomatoes which are half dried or 'mi-cuit' (also known fancifully as 'sun-blush').

Tomato pastes and extracts are available, which are good added in small quantities to sauces or simply served with a knob of butter as a dressing for cooked pasta.

Herbs, Spices and Seasonings

The rule with herbs is to use them fresh whenever possible. The best thing to do is grow them yourself, either in the garden or in a windowbox, where feasible. You can then dry them for use in the winter, which will be infinitely better than the dried herbs you can buy (unless they are Italian!).

Oregano This is an exception to the general herb-drying rule, and it will keep well dried, in a jar. The plant, closely related to thyme, has a minty flavour and can be found almost anywhere in the Italian hills. It is much beloved of the southern Italians, who use it mainly in pizzas, but also in dishes cooked 'alla pizzaiola'.

Basil In Italy we consider basil to be the king of aromatic herbs, and in my view its culinary value is far superior to all the others. It has a refreshing and distinctive quality which can perk up and enliven even the simplest of tomato sauces.

It is such a shame that basil is only really available in summer, although I do know some green-fingered enthusiasts who have managed to keep plants going for longer by cultivating them carefully inside, and using the precious leaves very parsimoniously. Dried basil should never be used as a substitute for fresh.

There are a trio of ways in which you can preserve basil, so that you can enjoy it out of season. One is to preserve a good bunch of leaves in oil, to which they will impart their fragrance. Another method, ideal for sauces, consists of chopping the basil coarsely and incorporating it in a pat of soft butter which is then frozen wrapped in foil. If you freeze the basil butter in a cylinder no thicker than a thin rolling pin, it will be easy to chip pieces off the block when the need arises rather than having to thaw the whole lot. Or you could make pesto. Although this does not last all that long, even covered with oil in the fridge, you could freeze it in ice-cube trays, to be instantaneously available whenever needed.

Rosemary This plant is typical of the Mediterranean, but succeeds in growing almost anywhere, because it is quite hardy. A twig will endow any roast with a distinctive yet delicate flavour, and will counterbalance fattier ingredients: but don't overdo the amount used.

Mint An institution in Britain cooked with peas or new potatoes, or in the sauce served with lamb. Italians generally attach less importance to it, simply sprinkling it raw over salads. It's a favourite taste of mine, however, and I perhaps use it more in my recipes than do most of my countrymen.

Parsley Ubiquitous it may be but the flavour and decorative quality of this herb are second-to-none. Try to use the continental flat-leaf variety rather than the curly parsley, as it is richer and more pungent in flavour.

Sage This is significant in one or two distinctive recipes: it is vital in the simple sauce for calf's liver, for instance.

Nutmeg This is a vital ingredient in many Italian dishes, particularly those containing spinach and ricotta, whether sweet or savoury. Don't buy ground nutmeg: always grate it freshly as you need it. This is why my recipes deliberately list among the ingredients '3 or 4 grates of nutmeg'.

Salt and pepper These should be added entirely to taste, and tasting is vitally important when you are cooking. For preference I would use a sea salt, and the pepper, whether white or black, must always be freshly ground. It's only in Britain that pepper is ground over virtually everything. In Italy, we only use pepper when it is strictly necessary. (Incidentally, according to Elizabeth David, the large pepper mills so ostentatiously presented to customers in most Italian restaurants are not used because they grind better: it's because the small ones were being stolen!)

Garlic Indispensable in Italian cooking, a clove or two imparting subtle flavouring to countless soups and sauces,

while greater quantities are responsible for the famous *Bagna Cauda* and (with basil) *Pesto alla Genovese*.

In spite of its reputation in myth and medicine from the Ancient Romans to the present day, one must not get carried away: garlic must be used above all in moderation, and at the right moment. If you are preparing a dish that needs only a hint of the flavour, you can chop a couple of cloves finely and leave them to macerate in some olive oil; strain this oil to use in your recipe. Or, if you want a hint of garlic in a salad, simply rub the inside of the salad bowl with a halved clove. You can do the same with a piece of toast, or bruschetta: before adding another topping, you can rub the toast lightly with a halved garlic clove. Delicious.

The cooking of garlic must always be moderate, even minimal, and it must never become brown or burned as the flavour becomes bitter, and ruins any food cooked with it.

Onion Together with garlic, onions constitute the basis of many Italian sauces, usually forming part of what is called 'soffritto'. Unlike garlic, onion can be cooked for a long time, and can actually be cooked up to the point when it becomes slightly caramelised. The cooking should be gentle, though.

Vinegar The Italians cook with quite a variety of vinegars. The most common is a strong white wine or red wine vinegar, of at least 6 per cent acidity, which is used to flavour quite a number of dishes besides salads. There are also a number of fruit vinegars. 'Aspretti' are widely available, the best known being that of peaches. Plum, raspberry and strawberry vinegars are generally made to flavour sauces, but also to highlight the flavours of fruit salads and sorbets.

The best-known Italian vinegar has to be balsamic, now famous all over the world. This precious vinegar is usually made in the region of Emilia Romagna, around the town of Modena. It is made from the reduced juices or must of the Trebbiano grape, which is called 'saba' or 'vino cotto'. This becomes thick and brown, and the taste is sweetish and very grapey. It is used in this form as an addition to sauces, to biscuits and tarts, or to make sorbets.

The most expensive balsamic vinegar is the result of up to fifty years' storage in wooden barrels. In this time an initial 100 litres of liquid will have reduced to about 5 litres of balsamic vinegar made in the 'Tradizionale' way – and you can appreciate why it is so expensive!

However, cheaper and younger balsamics are also available, which have been aged for from five up to twenty years. They lack the classification 'Tradizionale' on the label. These are useful in general cooking.

Anchovies As well as being eaten as antipasti, preserved anchovies are an important constituent of sauces and a flavouring for other dishes. They reach their apotheosis in *Bagna Cauda*. The best way to buy them is in their salted form: Italian delicatessens sell them in bulk from large tins. The flesh should be pink and fresh smelling, and you should choose medium-sized ones, as the larger ones have a coarser taste. Soak them for 30 minutes to desalt them, then you have to dry them and fillet them (the bones are still attached). When they are dried and filleted, you can preserve them in olive oil for use whenever you need them. Keep in the fridge.

Anchovy fillets canned in oil are widely available, and can be used in many recipes.

Capers Choose salted ones rather than those preserved in vinegar, which retain their vinegar flavour. You will need to desalt them before use by soaking for 30 minutes in water, then draining them well. Try to buy smallish ones, and the best Italian capers come from Pantelleria and Lipari.

Mushrooms

For a few weeks in autumn wild mushrooms can be found in profusion by anyone who knows where to look. Out of season their indispensable contribution to recipes has to be achieved by more roundabout means. While they are abundant, either preserve them (see the *Funghi sott'Olio* recipe), freeze them, when their thawed texture will be acceptable in sauces, or dry them. Dried mushrooms are readily available from delicatessens too. They are easily regenerated for use in sauces by being soaked in lukewarm water for 10–15 minutes before use. (And always keep and use the soaking water, as this will be wonderfully flavoured.) A small amount, just 25g (1 oz), of dried ceps or porcini will improve the flavour of 450g (1 lb) ordinary field mushrooms. Keep some dried mushrooms in the fridge.

Ceps Known in Italy as porcini, in France as cèpes, ceps are members of the genus *Boletus*. Most readily available dried, but you can occasionally find them in season (especially on the Continent) in markets and stores.

Truffles These are a combination of all the smells and the tastes of the world put together. Indescribable. Something you either love or you hate. So intense and so remarkable and so completely different from anything that you know. White truffles, which grow around Alba and Piedmont, are more powerful than the black ones. You couldn't travel on a train or plane with a truffle, so intense is the smell. Truffles grow in the ground by the roots of some trees. The best ones are those which grow near the hazelnut.

Truffles should be combined with the simplest of foods – with a basic risotto, a plain buttered dish of pasta, or on potato salad or baked eggs.

Cheeses

Although cheeses are more fully described in a chapter of their own, a word or two about the ones you are likely to use for cooking.

Parmesan Always buy it in a piece, never pre-grated in tubs or packets. Choose Parmesan that is a fine pale yellow, wrap it in foil or a damp cloth, and it will keep in the fridge for several weeks. Try to buy the genuine thing, which will have the stamp 'Parmigiano Reggiano' on the rind. Others, like Grana Padano, can be found and used instead.

Ricotta Always buy it perfectly sweet and fresh and use it straightaway. If kept too long at home (or in the shop), it quickly acquires an acid taste.

Mozzarella This must always be kept cool and damp in its whey, which is why it is always sold floating in liquid. If you buy more than is needed, preserve it in the fridge in a small amount of lightly salted water. Buy good Italian brands, especially those made from buffalo milk, rather than northern European imitations.

equipment

In an Italian kitchen, successful cooking does not depend on the tools you use, but tasks are made simpler with the aid of certain utensils and gadgets. Below are a few I think you should consider, but you will already have many other kitchen necessities such as baking trays, wooden spoons, pots and pans.

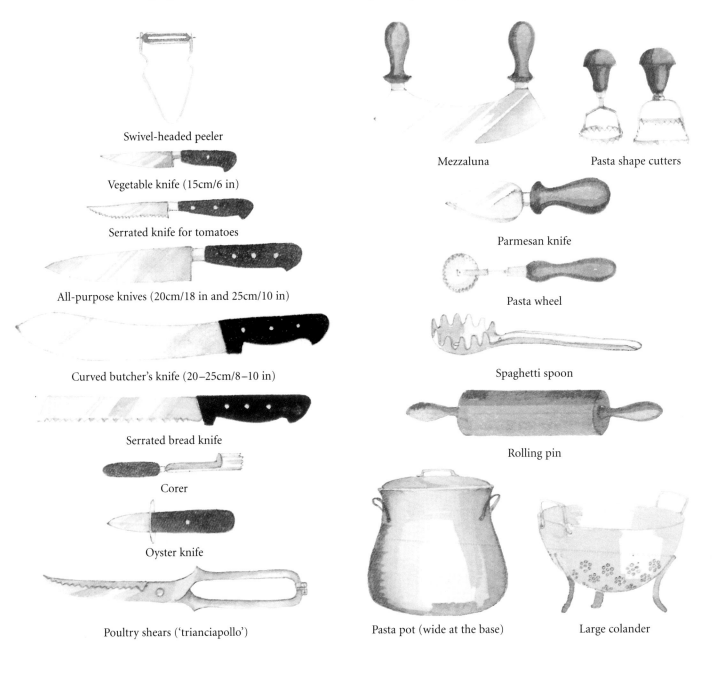

Swivel-headed peeler

Vegetable knife (15cm/6 in)

Serrated knife for tomatoes

All-purpose knives (20cm/18 in and 25cm/10 in)

Curved butcher's knife (20–25cm/8–10 in)

Serrated bread knife

Corer

Oyster knife

Poultry shears ('trianciapollo')

Mezzaluna

Pasta shape cutters

Parmesan knife

Pasta wheel

Spaghetti spoon

Rolling pin

Pasta pot (wide at the base)

Large colander

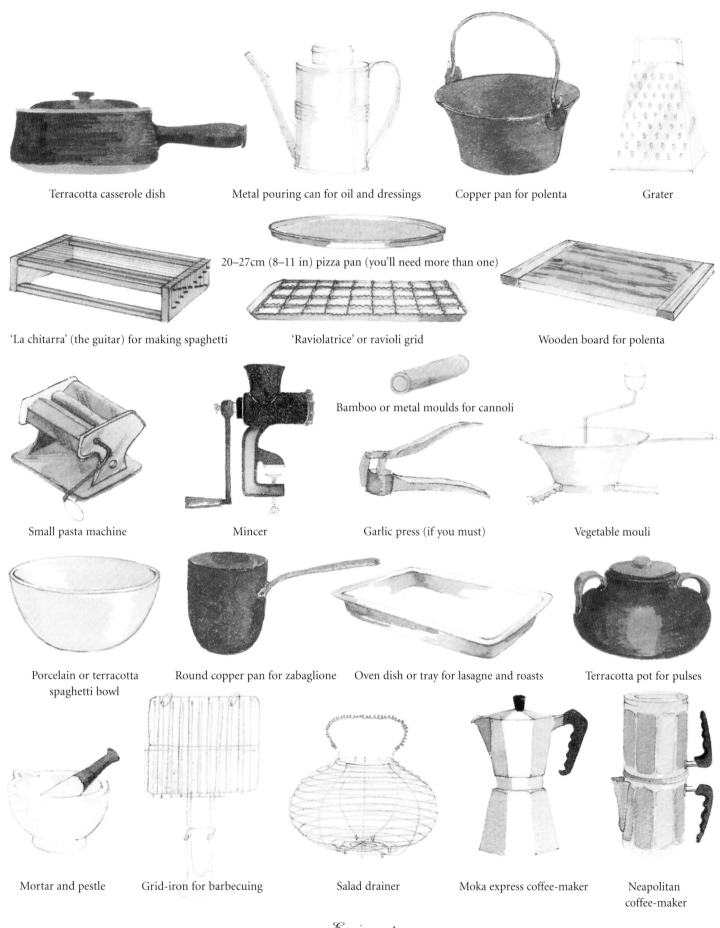

Terracotta casserole dish

Metal pouring can for oil and dressings

Copper pan for polenta

Grater

'La chitarra' (the guitar) for making spaghetti

20–27cm (8–11 in) pizza pan (you'll need more than one)

'Raviolatrice' or ravioli grid

Wooden board for polenta

Small pasta machine

Mincer

Bamboo or metal moulds for cannoli

Garlic press (if you must)

Vegetable mouli

Porcelain or terracotta spaghetti bowl

Round copper pan for zabaglione

Oven dish or tray for lasagne and roasts

Terracotta pot for pulses

Mortar and pestle

Grid-iron for barbecuing

Salad drainer

Moka express coffee-maker

Neapolitan coffee-maker

Antipasti
starters

There is a popular misconception that the word 'antipasto' means the course that is eaten before the pasta dish. Rather, it is the food served before the 'pasto', or meal, begins and its purpose is to 'stuzzicare l'appetito', to stimulate the appetite. The attitude to the course varies enormously from region to region. The southern Italians tend to miss it out altogether, preferring to jump straight into 'il primo', the first course, while in the north, and particularly in Piedmont where I grew up, there are literally thousands of local variations.

Opposite: A typical antipasto spread, including *Carciofi sott'Olio* (cooked as for *Funghi sott'Olio*, see page 29), *Giardiniera* (page 32) and *Acciughe in Salsa Verde* (page 23).

You might have one or two thin slices of salami or Parma ham with pickles (my own favourite is porcini sott'olio), or a selection of meats and sausages – perhaps salame felino from Emilia, prosciutto San Daniele, a pork sausage called sopressata from Calabria, and mucetta (dried fillet of chamois) from the Aosta valley. Mortadella will be served in its native Bologna, and bresaola in the Valtellina in Lombardy. By the sea you'll find tiny fish fried in oil or marinated raw. In Tuscany a plate of young beans will be seasoned with a fruity olive oil, or there will be all sorts of crostini. Up in the mountains there will be autumn salads of raw porcini or fine slices of wild boar served with a little olive oil and lemon juice. Usually the antipasto will be mildly acidic in order to stimulate the gastric juices.

All the recipes I have given here can be eaten by themselves. (Some, of course, can be expanded into a main course by increasing the quantities: vegetable antipasti often make good accompaniments to the fish and meat dishes in il primo – there is no hard-and-fast rule, and the chapters overlap.) If you particularly want to impress, you can combine three or four antipasto dishes. In either case, the quantities served will be small.

Acciughe Ripiene al Forno
baked stuffed anchovies

6 The fresh anchovy is undoubtedly one of the most popular fish in Italy. The best are to be found around Salerno and the coastlines of Sicily. Because they are so sought after, they command quite a high price. The Ligurian Gulf is also famous for anchovies, where the locals have established a proper cottage industry, salting and preserving the fish as fillets.
Each of the many coastal villages and cities has its own recipe, and rapid transportation means that even inland you can buy very fresh fish. 9

makes 12 'sandwiches'

24 fresh anchovies

1 tbsp each of chopped fresh dill, flat-leaf parsley, chives and rosemary

a few fresh sage leaves, finely chopped

1 garlic clove, chopped

25g (1 oz) pine nuts, or chopped walnuts

2–3 tbsp olive oil

a few drops of lemon juice

10g (¼ oz) fresh breadcrumbs

salt and pepper to taste

In countries where fresh anchovies are not available, you can use frozen ones instead. Fresh or frozen sardines can also be used, but since these are larger than anchovies, you will need only half as many.

Preheat the oven to 220°C/425°F/Gas 7, and grease a baking tray with a little olive oil.

With a pair of kitchen scissors, cut off the heads, tails and lower parts of the anchovies, and discard the innards. Using your thumb, loosen the backbone from the flesh, leaving the two fillets still attached by the upper skin. Wash and dry the fish.

Chop the herbs and garlic finely together and mix with the pine nuts and a tbsp of olive oil. Lay 12 of the anchovies skin side down next to each other in the greased tray. Spread a little of the herb mixture on each, season with salt and pepper, sprinkle with lemon juice and cover with another anchovy, skin side up, to make a 'sandwich'. Sprinkle with breadcrumbs and pour on the remaining olive oil in a thin stream. Bake for 8–10 minutes in the preheated oven until golden. Serve hot or cold.

Two anchovy 'sandwiches' per person make an antipasto; four would be sufficient for a main course.

Acciughe in Salsa Verde
anchovy fillets in green sauce

> ❝ Perhaps more than any other, this recipe reminds me of my youth, as Piedmont is the region where it is most liked and eaten. Some friends and I would go on outings into the mountains or to nearby villages, and we would invariably end up in a small inn or café for lunch. Here we would devour huge quantities of anchovies in green sauce, served with slices of home-made salami and slices of succulent fresh bread, all washed down with a locally produced Barbera wine. Few meals have remained so clearly in my mind! ❞

fills a 500ml (18 fl oz) jar

1 x 350g (12 oz) can anchovy fillets in oil

1 garlic clove

a large bunch of fresh flat-leaf parsley

2 dried red chillies

the inside of a white bread roll, or 25g (1 oz) fresh breadcrumbs

1 tbsp white wine vinegar

at least 150ml (5 fl oz) olive oil

For this antipasto, the ideal anchovies would be the salted kind, which need rinsing and filleting first. But you can use fillets canned in oil, provided they are of good quality, like the Sicilian ones. Two or three fillets per person would be enough for a starter with fresh bread, perhaps eaten together with other antipasti.

Open the can of anchovies, drain off the oil, and set aside. Finely chop the garlic, parsley and chillies. Soak the bread in the vinegar, squeeze and finely chop. Mix these latter ingredients together.

In a glass jar with a rubber seal, place first a layer of the herb mixture and then a layer of anchovies; cover with oil and press down. Repeat until the jar is full. Pour some olive oil over the top – the anchovies must be completely covered – and keep in the fridge until required (but no longer than a week, because the oil does not preserve the parsley).

Anguilla in Carpione
marinated eel

> ❝ A typical Roman and Neapolitan Christmas dish is "capitone", a type of eel that is first roasted, usually on a barbecue, and then marinated. Capitone are large, caught when they have spent a year or so in river estuaries before embarking on the long journey to the Sargasso Sea to spawn. The fresh eels that are normally found in the market are generally quite small, and are rather tastier. ❞

serves 4

500g (1 lb 2 oz) eel, cleaned and skinned (get the fishmonger to do this for you)

olive oil for brushing

salt and pepper to taste

Marinade

2 tbsp olive oil

1 tbsp white wine vinegar

1 garlic clove, coarsely chopped

6 fresh bay leaves

Cut the eel up into chunks 10cm (4 in) long, brush with olive oil and season with salt and pepper. Grill, preferably over charcoal, until cooked or even slightly burned on the outside, making sure the flesh remains firm. (You could eat it now, delicious with slices of lemon.)

While the eel is cooling, mix the marinade ingredients together and season with salt and pepper. Turn the pieces of eel over in the marinade so that they are well covered. Leave to marinate in the fridge for at least 24 hours in order to maximise the flavour (and up to a couple of days).

There are some 1,000 or so recipes for eel in the Veneto, the area around Venice, where the lagoons abound in this fish.

Cozze al Forno
baked mussels

serves 4

500g (1 lb 2 oz) fresh mussels (about 12 per person)

1 garlic clove, finely chopped

2 tbsp finely chopped fresh flat-leaf parsley

2 tbsp dry breadcrumbs, or 25g (1 oz) fresh

1 tbsp olive oil

salt and pepper to taste

❛This recipe is popular in many parts of Italy, and is very easy to prepare. It can also be served as a main course: simply increase the quantity of mussels. And because you are cooking with olive oil, the mussels can be eaten hot or cold.❜

Try and choose the biggest and freshest mussels, making sure that they are tightly closed and quite heavy.

Clean the mussels in a sink under running tap water. Throw away any that gape, and do not close when you tap them sharply, or any that float. Place the mussels in a lidded saucepan with about 150ml (5 fl oz) water, cover and bring to the boil. Shake the pan: the steam will open the mussels in a few minutes. (At this point throw away any that have not opened.) Put aside to cool.

Preheat the oven to 220°C/425°F/Gas 7.

Next, take off the top half of each shell. Loosen the mussels and arrange the lower shells next to one another in a baking dish. Sprinkle them with the garlic and parsley mixed together, then with the breadcrumbs, and season with salt and pepper. Finally pour a thin trickle of olive oil over each mussel. Then place the dish in the preheated oven for about 10 minutes. Serve hot or cold.

Insalata di Mare
seafood salad

> ❝ A variety of fish can appear in this salad. You need a shellfish of some kind, and some prawns or shrimps, but a cephalopod is vital – squid, cuttlefish or octopus – for both looks and texture. All the fish should be very fresh: frozen will not do. Look in your local fish market for inspiration, as the Italians do. Even the smallest coastal village in Italy has its own seafood salad, which is always based on seafood caught locally. ❞

serves 4

500g (1 lb 2 oz) mussels in their shells

350g (12 oz) squid

150g (5½ oz) giant prawns

2 scallops, about 140g (5 oz) flesh in total

juice of 1 lemon

3 tbsp olive oil

1 tbsp chopped fresh flat-leaf parsley

a small bunch of fresh chives, chopped

salt and pepper to taste

Serve along with other antipasti as a light summer main course.

Prepare and cook the mussels as in the previous recipe. When cool, remove the mussels from their shells.

To clean the squid, first of all pull the head and tentacles away from the tubular body. Strip off the outer transparent skin from the body, and remove and discard the internal 'bone'. Cut off the mouth and head, but keep the tentacles whole in bunches. Do not cut the body at this point. Keep the shells on the prawns (they will add flavour during cooking), but de-vein them.

Bring a saucepan of water to the boil and add some salt. Put in the squid, the prawns and the scallops. The cooking time depends on size, but all should be cooked within 5–8 minutes. Remove the prawns after 5 minutes; the squid too (if they are small ones) will be cooked in 5 minutes. Test for tenderness, and drain the fish when cooked. Cut the scallops in half and large squid into 1.5cm (¾ in) slices. Shell the prawns and cut them each into four. Mix the mussels with the other seafood and leave to cool.

When the seafood is cold, dress with the lemon juice and olive oil. Season with salt, pepper and parsley, and scatter the chives over the top.

Vitello Tonnato
veal in tuna sauce

serves 12 or more

1 piece veal steak, weighing about 1kg (2¼ lb)

1 carrot, chopped

2–3 celery stalks, cut in pieces

1 onion, halved

175g (6 oz) canned tuna in oil

2 tbsp capers in vinegar, plus a few extra for decoration

6 anchovy fillets

150g (5½ oz) mayonnaise, preferably home-made

12 or so baby gherkins (cornichons), sliced

salt and pepper to taste

6 This famous combination may seem rather unusual, but it makes for a really tasty dish. It is popular in all regions of Italy, but the Piedmontese version is perhaps the easiest. I have made a slight change to the classic recipe by incorporating the poached vegetables in the sauce, which I think adds extra interest and flavour. 9

The cut of veal used in Italy is the 'girello', or eye of silverside, which provides very fine, close-textured slices when cut across the grain.

Put the meat, carrot, celery and onion in a suitable pan, season with a pinch of salt, and cover with water. Bring to the boil, skim, than cover and simmer for around 1 hour. Leave to cool in the water, then drain, retaining the vegetables. Cut the veal into very thin slices and arrange on a platter.

Put the poached vegetables, tuna, capers and anchovies into the food processor and blend to produce a smooth paste the consistency of thick cream. Mix this with the mayonnaise, and season with salt and pepper.

Spread the tuna paste over the veal slices, and decorate the top with the sliced gherkins and the reserved extra capers.

Funghi Ripieni
stuffed mushrooms

> For the recipe you can use open cultivated mushrooms or field mushrooms. The stuffing need not be exactly as I suggest, but can vary according to imagination and the ingredients to hand.

serves 4

4 large open mushrooms

1 egg

1 small ripe tomato, skinned and chopped

25g (1 oz) fresh bread

4 tbsp freshly grated Parmesan

1 garlic clove, chopped

1 tbsp finely chopped fresh flat-leaf parsley

1 tbsp olive oil

1 tbsp dry breadcrumbs

salt and pepper to taste

Preheat the oven to 220°C/425°F/Gas 7.

Clean the mushrooms. Detach the stalks and chop them coarsely.

To prepare the filling, first beat the egg and mix it with the chopped mushroom stalks, the chopped tomato, the roughly broken-up bread, the Parmesan, garlic, parsley, salt and pepper and finally 1 tsp of the olive oil. Mix well together and use to fill the mushroom caps.

Oil a baking dish and in it place the mushrooms side by side. Sprinkle the dry breadcrumbs over the mushrooms and trickle with the remaining oil. Bake in the preheated oven for 20 minutes until golden brown on top. Eat hot or cold.

Funghi sott'Olio
mushrooms in oil

6 Imagine a fine autumn day. You have managed to pick a basket full of beautiful, small, good-quality ceps. Most of them will be used right away, perhaps in a risotto; some can be sliced and dried. My suggestion for the remainder would be to cook them in vinegar and water, preserve them in oil, and to serve them as an hors d'oeuvre at Christmas, or in any antipasto misto. 9

fills a 1 litre (1¾ pint) jar

1kg (2¼ lb) ceps (or button mushrooms)

700ml (1¼ pints) white wine vinegar

100ml (3½ fl oz) white wine

200ml (7 fl oz) water

4 bay leaves

10 cloves

2 tbsp salt

olive oil to cover

3 garlic cloves, halved

But for those who don't have access to fresh ceps, the recipe can be recreated using ordinary button mushrooms. The flavour won't be the same, of course, but they will still taste good.

Clean the mushrooms thoroughly, discarding any that are not firm. In a saucepan large enough to take the mushrooms, bring the vinegar, wine and water to the boil. Add the bay leaves, cloves, salt and mushrooms. Bring back to the boil and simmer for 6–8 minutes; the mushrooms tend to float so you have to push them down with a spoon while they are cooking. They will lose water as they cook, and reduce in volume. Drain and, without touching the mushrooms with your hands, put them to cool and dry on a clean cloth, stem side down so that no liquid can be trapped.

Sterilise a l litre (1¾ pint) preserving jar and pour a little olive oil into the bottom. Using a spoon, put in a layer of mushrooms, 1 bay leaf and a half garlic clove, cover with oil and proceed in this way up the jar, pressing the mushrooms into spaces to make sure no air is trapped. The oil must cover the final layer of mushrooms. They will keep for a long time – unless, of course, you are tempted to eat them straightaway!

Make carciofini sott'olio in the same way using 1.3kg (3lb) fresh small artichokes.

Fiori di Zucchini Ripieni
stuffed courgette flowers

> This is a classic summer recipe, eaten when the courgette flowers are, briefly, in season. In Italy, the flowers are sold in all the markets, usually by little old ladies who offer them in special baskets called "cavagne", along with herbs and other garden produce. You can grow them yourself at home, or try to persuade a gardening friend to let you have a few from time to time. They can occasionally be found in specialist vegetable shops, but most of the crop in Britain goes straight to the restaurant trade.

serves 4

12 courgette flowers

olive oil for frying (see right)

Batter

2 eggs

55g (2 oz) plain flour

4 tbsp cold water

If the flower is female, and comes with a small courgette attached, then you should deep-fry. If the flower is thin and alone (male!), then shallow-fry.

First make the batter. Beat the eggs, stir in the flour evenly, then gradually add the water to make a smooth consistency. Put the batter aside.

Meanwhile, clean the flowers carefully: gently wash and dry the outside, and make sure there are no insects inside.

Prepare the stuffing by mixing thoroughly together the ricotta, salt, pepper, nutmeg, chives, egg and Parmesan. Use spoonfuls of this mixture to fill the flowers.

Dip the flowers into the batter and fry in the hot oil until golden brown. Drain on kitchen paper briefly before serving as soon as you can.

Stuffing

250g (9 oz) fresh ricotta cheese

3 grates of nutmeg

a bunch of fresh chives, chopped

1 egg, beaten

4 tbsp freshly grated Parmesan

salt and pepper to taste

Giardiniera
pickled garden vegetables

> ❝ Pickles have an important role to play in the Italian meal. They both tease the appetite and stimulate the gastric juices into greater activity. In a mixed hors d'oeuvre or antipasto misto, there is nearly always something slightly vinegary. ❞

fills a 2.8 litre (5 pint) preserving jar

2 turnips, about 250g (9 oz)

4 large carrots, about 450g (1 lb)

1 celeriac, about 500g (1 lb 2 oz)

1 red sweet pepper, about 250g (9 oz)

250g (9 oz) broccoli or cauliflower florets

4 celery stalks, about 150g (5½ oz)

115g (4 oz) green French beans

55g (2 oz) mangetout

150g (5½ oz) small white onions

about 1.2 litres (2 pints) white wine vinegar

2–3 small sprays fresh bay leaves, washed

2 tsp black peppercorns

3–4 large garlic cloves, sliced

salt to taste

Wash and peel the turnips, carrots and celeriac. Wash and cut into quarters the red pepper, removing all the seeds and pith. Separate the broccoli or cauliflower into medium florets and wash them. Trim the celery, and top and tail the beans and mangetout. Peel the onions. Cut the root vegetables into 1cm (½ in) thick slices, using a special crinkle-edged cutter. Halve the beans and mangetout, and cut the celery into chunks.

Bring a large saucepan of water to the boil, add a little salt, and put in the celeriac, carrot and turnip first. Allow to boil for 10 minutes, then add the remaining vegetables and simmer for about 5–6 more minutes. They should all be cooked to al dente, not soft. Drain and lay them out to dry on a clean cloth, doing so with tongs rather than your hands.

Meanwhile, wash and thoroughly dry your preserving jars.

When the vegetables are completely dry, pour a little of the vinegar into the bottom of the jar, put in a spray of bay leaves and then start to fill up with your vegetables, using a spoon as it is important not to touch the vegetables after they have been cooked. As you fill the jar, place the peppercorns, slices of garlic and bay leaves among the vegetables. Fill up with the vinegar as you progress, making sure you have no air trapped between. The vinegar should completely cover all the vegetables. Seal the jar and keep for at least three months before using.

oven-dried tomatoes

makes about 450g
(1 lb)

1kg (2¼ lb) ripe plum tomatoes,
cut in half

20g (¾ oz) salt

1 tbsp dried oregano

6 tbsp extra virgin olive oil

20 fresh basil leaves, shredded

❝ Sun-dried tomatoes have had great success among gourmets all over the world in the last few years, but have been known in Italy for much longer. The idea is to have tomatoes all year round, and to dehydrate them so that they can be preserved. For this, you need very ripe tomatoes and a lot of sun, which is easy in Italy. To do the same yourself in Britain, you need to use a different method, using the oven rather than the sun. ❞

The tomatoes will not keep for long, so must be eaten soon after making, but they are wonderful for antipasto, in salads and sauces.

Preheat the oven to about 70°C/160°F/the very lowest gas possible.

Place the tomato halves on to a baking tray and sprinkle with the salt and dried oregano. Cook in the preheated oven until most of the moisture has evaporated. Make sure the heat isn't too high, as you only want to dry out the tomatoes, not 'cook' them. After 2–3 hours of slow drying, add the olive oil and bake for another hour.

Leave to cool, then add the basil leaves just before serving.

Insalata di Peperoni Arrostiti
roast pepper salad

serves 6

4 fleshy yellow and red sweet peppers

2 garlic cloves, coarsely chopped

3 tbsp olive oil

1 tbsp coarsely chopped fresh flat-leaf parsley

salt to taste

❝ This is without doubt one of my favourite recipes. It is an example of the way in which the flavour of sweet peppers can change completely according to whether they are fried or roasted, or indeed have their skins removed, as here. The peppers can be eaten by themselves, with some good bread, or as an accompaniment to meat dishes – especially pork. ❞

Roast the peppers over a barbecue – or over a gas burner – turning them frequently until black and blistered. Leave them to cool and then peel off the skin, which should come away quite easily if the peppers are well roasted. Remove the stalk, seeds and pith.

Cut the pepper flesh lengthways into narrow strips and place in a dish, adding the garlic. Dress with oil, parsley and salt. The dish can be eaten hot or cold, but improves with standing, and is excellent eaten the next day.

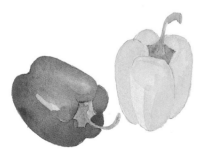

Zucchini alla Scapece
fried courgette salad

6 This is a typically Neapolitan method of dressing cooked greens and other vegetables, including aubergines, as well as anchovies. The origin of the dish is not quite certain, but is probably derived from the Spanish or Provençal "escabeche", which means to dress with a marinade of oil, vinegar and spices. It makes an excellent starter. 9

serves 6

1kg (2¼ lb) courgettes

vegetable oil for shallow-frying

a bunch of fresh mint

2 tbsp olive oil

1 tbsp white wine vinegar

1 garlic clove, coarsely sliced

salt to taste

Slice the courgettes 5mm (¼ in) thick, and fry them a few at a time in the hot vegetable oil in a pan until they are a good brown colour on both sides. Remove them from the pan, place them in a dish, and sprinkle with salt. Tear the mint leaves off the stalks, and scatter them whole among the courgettes. Add the olive oil, vinegar and slices of garlic, and mix well together. Leave to marinate for at least a couple of hours before serving to allow the flavours to develop fully.

Peperoni Gialli con Bagna Cauda
yellow peppers with bagna cauda

6 Even though Piedmont has no coast, anchovies play an important part in local gastronomy. Indeed, there is a valley in the province of Cuneo where the villagers occupy themselves almost exclusively with preserving this fish in salt. Of the many recipes using anchovies, this is one of my favourites: the distinctive flavour of the bagna cauda is juxtaposed with the sweet taste of the roasted peppers. This dish is excellent served hot or cold. 9

serves 4

2 fleshy yellow sweet peppers

Bagna cauda

8 garlic cloves, peeled

150ml (5 fl oz) milk

a nut of butter

20 anchovy fillets in oil, drained

4 tbsp double cream

Clean the peppers, removing the stalks, seeds and pith, and cut them into quarters. Put the garlic cloves in a pan with the milk and cook gently until soft, about 35 minutes.

Preheat the oven to 220°C/425°F/Gas 7.

Add the nut of butter and the anchovies to the garlic and reduced milk in the pan. Stir and let the mixture slowly dissolve over a low heat until a paste is produced. Pass it through a sieve, then add the cream.

Place the pepper pieces on a greased dish and put them in the preheated oven for 15 minutes. Remove from the oven and turn the heat down to 190°C/375°F/Gas 5. Fill each piece of pepper with some of the paste and put back into the oven for a further 5 or so minutes, until the peppers go brown at the edges.

Il Primo
the first course

Il primo is the first 'real' course in the Italian meal. Traditionally, it was the 'filler', and on rare occasions the whole meal would be pared down to this one course.

There are some wonderful soups in the Italian repertoire. Each coastal region has its own distinctive fish soup, and there is an infinite variety of vegetable soups. Rice may be added in the north, pasta in the south and beans in central Italy; in Liguria the soup might be predominantly green and give off the heady fragrance of pesto, while around Naples it will be based on tomatoes, onions and garlic.

The glorious pasta dishes Italy is so famous for range from the simplest – spaghetti tossed in garlic and olive oil or in a lightly cooked tomato sauce – to complicated baked lasagnes and stuffed pasta like tortelloni and ravioli. Then there are gnocchi, a type of pasta dumpling made from a potato or maize flour paste.

Risotto is a northern speciality. Simple vegetable risottos are made with asparagus or ceps, while the Venetians like to add clams and mussels. For a special occasion, the risotto may be decorated with slivers of white truffles, as is the custom in Piedmont.

Another dish from the north is polenta. It can be fried or baked, eaten with simple sauces, and used instead of bread to accompany meat and poultry. So it is really impossible to classify simply as a first course, although it's often eaten as one.

I have also included pizza recipes in this section, although they too defy strict classification, usually being served by themselves, rather than as part of a meal. Any of these dishes, in fact, makes an excellent lunch or light supper, accompanied by a salad and a bottle of wine, and followed by a good cheese, home-made bread and some fresh fruit.

Opposite: *Risotto con Porcini* (see page 49).

beef or chicken stock

> ❛ Beef or chicken stocks form the basis of most Italian minestre and thick soups, risottos and other dishes. One of the most classic of Italian soups, "pastina in brodo", consists of nothing more than a good stock in which small pastas such as stelline – or small stuffed shapes – are cooked. A sprinkling of Parmesan is the final touch. And the equally famous stracciatella whisks eggs into stock, along with fresh herbs. ❜

makes about 3 litres (5¼ pints) stock

1kg (2¼ lb) stewing beef and some bones, or 1 chicken of about 2kg (4½ lb), or half and half according to taste

4 litres (7 pints) water

2 carrots, cut in pieces

1 onion, halved

2–3 celery stalks, roughly chopped

4 bay leaves

1 tbsp black peppercorns

salt to taste

A beef stock should be made from the meat of a mature animal, and a bone with marrow can be added if you want to thicken the broth, for example when making consommés. If the full flavour of the beef is to be savoured in the stock, it is advisable to mince the meat first. Choose a piece of silverside, brisket or topside if you are going to use the meat for a dish on its own, such as boiled beef salad.

For the chicken stock you should choose a bird which is neither too old nor too young. The cooked chicken can itself be used in other recipes if liked.

Immerse the meat in the lightly salted water in a large saucepan and bring to the boil. Skim off the froth and add the remaining ingredients. Bring back to the boil and allow to simmer for 2–3 hours if using beef, slightly less for chicken. Strain, remove fat, and chill or freeze.

Brodo di Pesce
fish stock

makes about 2.2 litres
(4 pints) stock

1.2kg (2¼–4½ lb) mixed fish
pieces (heads, bones etc.)

4 litres (7 pints) water

2–3 celery stalks, roughly
chopped

2 carrots, cut in pieces

a bunch of fresh flat-leaf parsley

1 onion, halved

2 garlic cloves

1 tsp fennel seeds

salt and pepper to taste

❛ Fish stock forms the basis of a number of soups
and seafood risottos, is simple to make and is
excellent value for money. If left to cool down,
fish stock tends to set into a jelly. ❜

More or less any part of a fresh fish is useful in the making of
stock. Try to cultivate your local fishmonger who will be able
to supply you with the heads of larger fish, which are normally
not sold. Use the heads and bones of white, rather than oily,
fish.

  Wash the pieces of fish under cold running water, then place
in a saucepan with the lightly salted water. Bring to the boil and
skim away the froth. Add all the remaining ingredients, and
leave to simmer for an hour. Strain the liquid through a sieve,
then allow to cool. Keep for a couple of days in the refrigerator,
or freeze.

Zuppa di Pesce
fish soup

> This recipe of mine is merely one version of the hundreds of fish soups that can be found in all Italian coastal towns, and is usually called "brodetto". It is a dish that can be tasty even if you have only a couple of kinds of fish to choose from. Monkfish, prawns and even mussels are ideal for this soup as they have a good flavour and do not disintegrate when cooked. For an even tastier soup you may well wish to include some heads of the larger fish, as I suggest in the recipe for fish stock. If you increase the proportions of fish, this soup can even become a main course.

serves 4

4 tbsp olive oil

1 large shallot or onion, chopped

1 carrot, chopped

1 celery stalk, chopped

75ml (2½ fl oz) dry white wine

8 prawns

20 mussels

250g (9 oz) monkfish, cut into pieces, or substitute with 8 scallops

750ml (25 fl oz) *Fish Stock* (see page 41)

1 garlic clove

8 small slices bread, freshly toasted

25g (1 oz) butter

1 tbsp chopped fresh flat-leaf parsley

salt and pepper to taste

Put the oil in a large pan and fry the shallot or onion together with the carrot and celery until the onion becomes golden and soft. Pour in the wine, bring to the boil, and allow to evaporate for 1 minute. Add all the fish and the stock and simmer for 10 minutes. Remove the heads and shells from the prawns and shell the mussels. Return the prawns and mussels to the soup. Taste for seasoning.

Lightly rub the garlic clove over the toast, then butter the toast. Place two slices in the bottom of each soup bowl. Pour in the soup, sprinkle with the parsley and serve straightaway.

Crema di Funghi Porcini
wild mushroom soup

serves 4

500g (1 lb 2 oz) fresh ceps, or 500g (1 lb 2 oz) field mushrooms, plus 25g (1 oz) dried porcini

1 medium onion, finely chopped

4 tbsp olive oil

1 litre (1¾ pints) *Beef Stock* (see page 40)

4 tbsp double cream

salt and pepper to taste

6 Simply handling the main ingredients for this soup – wild mushrooms – fills me with ecstasy and reminds me always of autumnal walks in beautiful woods in search of them. This soup can be made in two ways, both of which are delicious. At the Neal Street Restaurant, I serve the version made with fresh ceps, and it is still, some twenty years later, one of the most popular items on the menu. (During the rest of the year I make it with ceps I have frozen.) The alternative version is even simpler, and (unless you have gathered your own ceps) cheaper. 9

If you are using fresh ceps, clean them and cut them into pieces. Cook the onion in the oil for 3–4 minutes, then add the ceps and sauté them for 6–7 minutes. Add the stock, bring to the boil and simmer for 20 minutes.

If you are not using fresh ceps, soak the dried porcini in lukewarm water for 10 minutes. Meanwhile, fry the field mushrooms together with the onion and then add the soaked porcini with their water and the stock. Simmer for about half an hour.

To finish either method, take the pan from the heat and blend the contents. Then return the soup to the pan, add the cream, salt and pepper and heat slowly. Remove from the heat before it boils, and serve hot.

To make croûtons, simply cut the bread into little cubes and fry in the butter until crisp and golden.

Croûtons

2 slices white bread

a nut of butter

Zuppa di Asparagi
cream of asparagus soup

serves 6

1kg (2¼ lb) asparagus

55g (2 oz) butter

1 small onion, finely chopped

1.7 litres (3 pints) water

1 large floury potato, peeled and cubed

40g (1½ oz) Parmesan, freshly grated

salt and pepper to taste

❛ Ideally this soup should be made with the wild asparagus that grows along the sunny roads of southern Italy in the springtime. However, you can use the larger, tender, dark green asparagus cultivated in Piedmont and Britain. The flavourful thin stalks known as sprue, and available early on in the British season, would be good. ❜

Trim and peel the asparagus if necessary. Chop the stalks into chunks, but cut off and reserve the tender tips.

Melt the butter in a large saucepan, add the onion, and leave to soften for a few minutes. Pour in the water, bring to the boil, then add the asparagus stalks and the potato cubes. Simmer until the potato is tender, about 15 minutes, then season with salt and pepper. Cook the asparagus tips separately until al dente in a little salted water.

Put the asparagus and potato mixture into a blender and reduce to a creamy consistency. Add the Parmesan, and check the seasoning. Serve the soup hot, with the asparagus tips divided between the individual serving plates.

Minestrone
vegetable soup

serves 4

8 tbsp olive oil

1 small onion, chopped

a good 250g (9 oz) prosciutto scraps

1.7 litres (3 pints) water

a total of 1.5kg (3 lb 5 oz) vegetables, made up of any or all of the following: carrots, celery, courgettes, cauliflower, potatoes, fresh peas, beetroot, garlic, leeks, Brussels sprouts, parsnips, marrow

1 x 400g (14 oz) can borlotti beans, drained and rinsed (if you can find fresh, so much the better)

2 small tomatoes, skinned and chopped

115g (4 oz) tubettini pasta, fregola (a type of small-grained couscous from Sardinia), or rice

salt and pepper to taste

❛ The name of this famous soup derives from "minestra", meaning "soup". (In many parts of Italy minestra means "green".) It is found all over the country, and all the regions have their own variations, suffixed alla milanese, alla genovese, alla piemontese etc. ❜

Normally the soup is prepared with leftover vegetables, so to detail precise ingredients seems a little dictatorial to me! The listing should give you an idea. What is important, though, is to use some Parma ham, the flavour of which is essential to the success of any minestrone. You can ask for bits and pieces of prosciutto from your Italian grocer or delicatessen: for example, the skin, the pieces cut out from around the bone, and the tail-end piece.

Heat the oil in a large saucepan. First fry the onion, then add the prosciutto pieces and the water, and let this simmer for an hour. Meanwhile, clean the vegetables as appropriate, then chop into cubes.

Discard the prosciutto pieces and add the vegetables to the pan, along with the drained beans, and continue to simmer. Add the tomatoes after a further 20 minutes. Cook for at least a further 30 minutes, after which time you should taste to see that all the vegetables are cooked, particularly the carrots. About 20 minutes or so before the dish is finished, add the pasta (or alternative), and cook until al dente.

Serve piping hot, sprinkled with the basil and Parmesan. Minestrone is also delicious cold.

To serve

a handful of fresh basil leaves

4 tbsp freshly grated Parmesan

basic risotto

serves 4

2 tbsp olive oil

55g (2 oz) butter

350g (12 oz) risotto rice

1.7 litres (3 pints) stock
(see page 40), simmering

55g (2 oz) Parmesan, freshly
grated

salt and pepper to taste

❛ *Oryza sativa,* the Latin name for rice, was first cultivated in Italy around the fifteenth century. The *japonica* subspecies forms a round and large grain, grown for its starchy qualities – indispensable when making risotto. The types include carnaroli, vialone nano, arborio and, less well known, baldo. ❜

Use a heavy saucepan with a rounded bottom, big enough to contain the rice, plus the liquid. Heat the oil and half the butter in this, then add and carefully coat the rice before adding any liquid. Turn the rice with a wooden spoon. You start to add the boiling stock when the rice is well and truly impregnated with butter and starts to stick to the bottom of the pan. Add only a ladleful at a time. Continue to stir and add the stock until the rice appears to be cooked (after 20–25 minutes).

At this stage remove the pan from the heat and, without stirring, let the rice absorb the last of the liquid. The risotto should have a creamy consistency, but the grains should still be firm to the bite (al dente). Just before serving (with the exception of seafood risottos), stir in the remaining butter and the freshly grated Parmesan. This last operation is called 'mantecare', possibly from the Spanish 'manteca' which means 'fat'. Taste finally for the right seasoning and serve straightaway. It is important to time the cooking so that this little work of art can be enjoyed and fully appreciated the moment the cheese has melted and the risotto is ready.

black risotto

serves 4

> ❝ This is a typically Venetian dish and is not always popular with everybody because of its slightly funereal appearance. It does, however, have an exceptional taste and is invariably to be found in all the renowned restaurants in Venice. ❞

500g (1 lb 2 oz) small cuttlefish, to make 300g (10½ oz) when cleaned

2 tbsp olive oil

55g (2 oz) butter

1 small onion, chopped

75ml (2½ fl oz) dry white wine

350g (12 oz) risotto rice

1.7 litres (3 pints) *Fish Stock* (see page 41), simmering

salt and pepper to taste

Not all seafood risottos need be 'black'. All round the Italian coast, risottos are made with the local fish and shellfish. Simply cook the shellfish briefly in water, which you then use as part of the risotto stock.

Clean the cuttlefish: first pull off the head with the tentacles, then pull out the rest of the contents of the body. Take out the backbone and remove the outside skin from the body, which should end up white. Find the small sac containing the ink, and put it to one side, taking care that it does not split. (You will recognise it by its bluish-silver colouring.) Discard the mouth and the eyes. Wash well, and then slice the tentacles and body into 1cm (½ in) pieces.

Melt the oil and half the butter together. Add the onion and cook gently until transparent. Then add the cut-up cuttlefish and continue to fry for at least another 5 minutes, until the cuttlefish has coloured. Add the wine and cook for another 5 minutes. Now pour in the rice, allow it to absorb the flavours for a couple of minutes, then gradually add the simmering fish stock as in the basic risotto method.

When the rice is nearly ready, add the ink from the cuttlefish sac to the last ladle of stock, and stir into the rice. Finish cooking and remove from the heat. Add the remaining butter, some salt and pepper to taste, stir, and serve hot.

Risotto con Porcini
mushroom risotto

> ❝ This dish is popular throughout northern Italy, especially in Piedmont, and together with truffle risotto and risotto nero, is one of my favourite dishes. I have reproduced it before, but it is such a classic that there is no way it could be omitted. ❞

serves 4

350g (12 oz) firm small fresh ceps, or 350g (12 oz) fresh button or field mushrooms plus 25g (1 oz) dried porcini

1 small onion, finely chopped

2 tbsp olive oil

55g (2 oz) butter

350g (12 oz) risotto rice

1.7 litres (3 pints) *Chicken Stock* (see page 40), simmering

55g (2 oz) Parmesan, freshly grated

salt and pepper to taste

Faced with the perennial problem of finding fresh ceps in generous quantities, you can use ordinary mushrooms plus a few dried porcini for extra taste. But this risotto is also eminently suitable for those wild mushrooms that you have gathered in season and then frozen.

Gently clean the ceps or other mushrooms, using a sharp knife and a brush (avoid washing them whenever possible). If you are using dried porcini, put them to soak in a small bowl of water for 15 minutes. Meanwhile, slice the fresh ceps or mushrooms.

Fry the onion in the oil and half the butter. When the onion begins to colour, add the sliced fresh mushrooms and continue to fry over a moderate heat for a couple of minutes. If using the dried porcini, chop them into small pieces and add to the mushrooms, keeping the water they soaked in to add to the risotto later with the stock. Add the rice and proceed according to the basic risotto method.

When the rice is al dente, remove from the heat, season and stir in the remaining butter and the Parmesan. Serve hot. (See the photograph on page 39.)

Risotto alla Milanese con Luganega
saffron risotto with sausage

6 Any rice dish that is described as "milanese" usually contains some saffron. Saffron rice is in itself a very delicate dish; the addition of luganega turns it into something rather more substantial. Luganega is fresh pork sausage that is sold by length (its name derives from the Greek "lukanika"). This typically Lombardian or Milanese product was usually made in the winter months when the household pig was killed, but nowadays it can be found all year round. It is made in a very long intestine 3cm (1¼ in) in diameter. You can use coarsely minced fresh pork instead, so long as you season it well. 9

serves 4

300g (10½ oz) luganega pork sausage, or fresh minced pork

4 grates of nutmeg (optional)

2 sachets powdered saffron, or 10 saffron strands

1 small onion, finely chopped

2 tbsp olive oil

55g (2 oz) butter

75ml (2½ fl oz) dry white wine

350g (12 oz) risotto rice

1.7 litres (3 pints) *Beef Stock* (see page 40), simmering

115g (4 oz) Parmesan, freshly grated

salt and pepper to taste

Remove the sausage skin and break the meat into pieces. If you are using fresh pork, season it with pepper, salt and nutmeg. If using saffron strands, toast them for a few seconds, but be careful not to burn them. Reduce them to a powder.

Fry the onion in the oil and half the butter, then add the sausage meat or the seasoned minced pork. After the onion has turned golden and the meat has browned, add the wine. Let this evaporate for a couple of minutes before pouring in the rice. You start to add the hot stock when the rice has absorbed all the butter and oil and when it begins to stick to the pan. Proceed now as for the basic risotto method, adding more salt, pepper and the saffron as you progress.

When the rice is al dente, incorporate the remaining butter and half the cheese. Serve with the rest of the grated cheese on top.

Risotto con Asparagi
asparagus risotto

serves 6

500g (1 lb 2 oz) fresh green asparagus (weighed after cleaning and trimming)

1.7 litres (3 pints) water (for cooking asparagus and for risotto)

1 small onion, thinly sliced

55g (2 oz) butter

350g (12 oz) risotto rice

55g (2 oz) Parmesan, freshly grated

salt and pepper to taste

❛ Perfect for vegetarians, other vegetable risotto dishes can be prepared in much the same way. Instead of asparagus, use vegetables that, when slightly overcooked, dissolve leaving a creaminess ideal for a risotto: broccoli, spinach, artichokes, marrow, courgettes, cauliflower. With some you can hold back a few choice pieces to decorate the cooked dish, just as asparagus tips are used here. To enhance the flavour of the rice, recycle the vegetable cooking water. ❜

Wash and peel the asparagus and cut away 3cm (1¼ in) or so of the hard white stalk at the bottom (use this and the skin to add flavour to the cooking water). Cut off about 5cm (2 in) of the tips and set them aside (as they are tender, they will need less cooking), and keep them intact for garnish. Boil the asparagus stalks with the trimmings in the water for 8–10 minutes, depending on thickness. When they are half cooked, add the tips. When fully cooked, strain the stock and keep it simmering. Separate out the asparagus tips and stalks and trimmings. Set the tips aside for garnish, and chop the stalks finely. Discard the trimmings.

Fry the onion in half the butter, then add the chopped asparagus and toss it for a couple of minutes. Now add the rice and proceed as for the basic risotto method, adding the hot broth until the rice is al dente and creamy, but not too stodgy. Remove from the heat and wait for a minute or two, then stir in the remaining butter, some salt and pepper, and the grated Parmesan. Serve in bowls, decorated with the asparagus tips.

basic polenta

serves 8

> ❝ My mother always used to make up a large batch of polenta, half of which was eaten immediately whilst still hot, and the rest kept in the larder ready to use when cold. The latter was then cut into slices, which were fried in butter or oil or grilled until crisp on each side. This was used to accompany meat dishes. Or it was broken into pieces and mixed together with tomato sauce, melting cheese and Parmesan, then baked in the oven until everything had melted together. ❞

1.7 litres (3 pints) salted water

300g (10½ oz) polenta flour, or 1 x 375g (13 oz) packet of bramata or instant polenta

55g (2 oz) butter

To finish

2 tbsp olive oil (for grilling) or a nut of butter or 4 tbsp olive oil (for frying)

Bring the salted water to the boil. Very carefully add the polenta flour, stirring constantly with a wooden spoon so that no lumps appear. You must continue to stir the polenta until you see that it starts to come away from the side of the saucepan. This will take only 5 minutes if you are using instant polenta, 30–40 minutes if you are using polenta flour or the classic bramata polenta. Now add the butter and stir in. Serve hot as an accompaniment, or leave to set, then cut into slices and grill or fry.

For the latter, rinse a deep rectangular dish with water, then pour the cooked polenta in and leave to set. When set, turn the polenta out on to a board and cut into 2cm (¾ in) thick slices (or use a metal wire that usually cuts cheese).

To grill, brush each slice with olive oil. Put under the preheated grill until it browns a little and forms a crust. To get nice criss-cross designs on the polenta, use a cast-iron griddle pan.

To fry, heat the oil or butter in a thick-bottomed pan. When hot, fry the slices of polenta on both sides until crisp and brown.

Polenta Concia
flavoured polenta

serves 4

❝ This flavoured polenta makes a delicious accompaniment to a stew of chicken, hare or beef, but I must admit that I am often tempted to eat it by itself! ❞

1.7 litres (3 pints) salted water

300g (10½ oz) polenta flour, or 1 x 375g (13 oz) packet of bramata or instant polenta

115g (4 oz) butter

115g (4 oz) Parmesan, freshly grated

115g (4 oz) fontina cheese, cut into chunks

Make the polenta as described on page 53, stirring until it starts to come away from the sides of the saucepan. When this happens, add the butter, the grated Parmesan and the chunks of fontina, stirring all the time until you see that all the ingredients have melted and are thoroughly mixed with the polenta. Serve directly on to heated plates with your own choice of stew.

Polenta con Funghi
polenta with wild mushrooms

serves 4

1.7 litres (3 pints) salted water

300g (10½ oz) polenta flour, or 1 x 375g (13 oz) packet of bramata or instant polenta

25g (1 oz) butter

55g (2 oz) Parmesan, freshly grated

6 This recipe reminds me of outings into the mountains made in my youth, invariably finishing up in some trattoria or other, where polenta with mushrooms would always be on the menu, especially in the autumn. The memory of this polenta, which would be prepared in a large copper pot over a wood fire, makes my mouth water even today. As elsewhere, you can substitute the ceps with ordinary field mushrooms combined with a few dried porcini to give extra flavour, or use a mixture of both wild and cultivated mushrooms. 9

For the sauce, clean and slice the fresh mushrooms, and soak the dried porcini for 15 minutes in lukewarm water. Fry the onion in the oil and butter, followed by the sliced fresh mushrooms and the drained dried porcini (save the soaking water). Cook together over a high heat for 10 minutes, then add the liquidised tomatoes and some of the porcini soaking water. Continue cooking for another 20 minutes so that the water from the tomatoes evaporates. When everything is fully cooked, add some salt, pepper and the basil leaves.

Make the basic polenta as on page 53, and when it is ready, add the butter and half the Parmesan. Serve in shallow bowls, pouring some of the wild mushroom sauce into the middle of each, and sprinkling the remaining Parmesan over the top (see photograph opposite).

For the sauce

350g (12 oz) fresh ceps, or 350g (12 oz) field mushrooms plus 25g (1 oz) dried porcini

1 small onion, chopped

3 tbsp olive oil

25g (1 oz) butter

1 x 225g (8 oz) can peeled plum tomatoes, liquidised, or polpa di pomodoro

6 fresh basil leaves, shredded

salt and pepper to taste

Pasta all'Uovo
basic pasta dough

makes 450g (1 lb)
pasta dough

300g (10½oz) plain flour

3 large, very fresh eggs

a generous pinch of salt

❝ The ideal proportions for the best home-made pasta dough are one large egg for every 115g (4 oz) flour, but variations in temperature and humidity as well as in the ingredients themselves may produce slightly different textures. You may need to vary the quantity of flour slightly: the thing to aim for is a dough which has been kneaded until it is perfectly smooth and elastic, yet firm. ❞

Pile the flour in a mound on a work surface. Break the eggs into the centre and add the salt. Stir the eggs into the flour, with a fork at first and then with your hands, until it forms a coarse paste. Add a little more flour if too moist.

Now the pasta dough has to be kneaded. It should be smooth and workable, not too soft but not too hard. Do this in the machine or by hand.

If the latter, clean your hands and the work surface first. Lightly flour the surface and your hands, and knead the dough with the heel or palm of one hand, pushing it away from you and folding it back towards you. Collect all the bits from the work surface and incorporate them into the dough. Flour the surface and your hands from time to time. After about 10–15 minutes the dough should be ready. Allow it to rest for 15–30 minutes before rolling, but cover with a cloth.

Once again, dust the clean work surface and the rolling pin with flour. Take a part of the dough (leaving the rest still covered), and begin to roll it out gently. Always roll away from you, each time rotating the dough by a quarter-turn.

The thickness required is dependent on the type of pasta:

1.5–2mm (¹⁄₁₆ in) for stuffed pasta, and 3–4mm (¹⁄₈ in) for lasagne and cannelloni. If you are making stuffed pasta such as ravioli, then use the pasta straightaway. If you are making lasagne, cut the sheets and place them on a floured cloth to dry a little. If you are cutting ribbons, fold the sheet of pasta into a loose roll and cut it into ribbons of the desired width. Open out the rolls gently and allow them to dry for a further 10 minutes or so before cooking.

If using a machine to roll the dough, you have to force a section of pasta dough through at a time until the dough becomes smooth. Then you decrease the gap each time through the rollers, so that the dough becomes thinner and longer. Repeat this until you obtain the desired thickness. Then either put it through the cutting rollers to make various sizes of ribbon, or cut into sheets.

Cook fresh pasta in a large saucepan, preferably with a rounded base. Use 1 litre (1¾ pints) water per 115g (4 oz) pasta, plus 2 tsp salt. When you put the pasta into the pot, give it a quick stir to prevent it from sticking together. (It is only with lasagne, which must be immersed one sheet at a time, that it is necessary to add a few drops of oil to the water.) Cooking time varies according to the kind of pasta, its thickness and whether it is stuffed, but home-made noodles and ribbons will take about 3–5 minutes. Stir the pasta while it is cooking, preferably with a long wooden fork. Always test the pasta when you think it should be almost done: it is ready when it is al dente, and slightly resistant. A little before it reaches that stage, take the saucepan off the heat, add a glass of cold water, and leave for a couple of seconds. Then drain the pasta and return immediately to the saucepan or a preheated dish, mixing it with a little sauce and perhaps some grated cheese. Serve it immediately.

tagliatelle with white truffles

> 6 One of the most popular and sought-after dishes in Alba is freshly made tagliatelle with white truffle, a combination of simple pasta with the sophisticated, rich taste of the truffle. Truffles are found from October through to the end of January in the district of Piedmont. They are highly prized – and highly priced. 9

serves 4

450g (1 lb) home-made tagliatelle (see page 56)

115g (4 oz) unsalted butter

55g (2 oz) Parmesan, freshly grated (preferably from a newly opened Parmigiano Reggiano)

1 small white truffle

salt and pepper to taste

Cook the tagliatelle al dente as usual, then drain, reserving a little of the cooking water. Toss in the butter and as much cooking water as you think it needs, then mix in the Parmesan. Season with salt and pepper. Present the tagliatelle to your guests served in separate warm plates. Shave the precious truffle directly on to each, and serve with a green salad including some wild rocket.

agnolotti with butter and sage

❝ "Agnolotti" is the Piedmontese name for ravioli, so the pasta is small and square in shape. Most of the work involved in this recipe consists of making the agnolotti themselves, so I have combined them with a very simple filling and sauce. ❞

serves 4

450g (1 lb) *Basic Pasta Dough* (see page 56)

55g (2 oz) Parmesan, freshly grated

salt and pepper to taste

Filling

250g (9 oz) Swiss chard or spinach

55g (2 oz) roast turkey or pork

55g (2 oz) mortadella slices

1 tbsp finely chopped fresh flat-leaf parsley

4 grates of nutmeg

Sauce

55g (2 oz) unsalted butter

10 fresh sage leaves

Make the pasta dough and keep it covered until you are ready to roll it out in sheets.

To make the filling, cook the Swiss chard (with its white stalks removed) or spinach in lightly salted water, then drain well, squeezing out all the water, and chop. Meanwhile, chop the meat and mortadella and mix together with the cooked chard or spinach, parsley, nutmeg, salt and black pepper. Thoroughly stir or blend the mixture.

To make the agnolotti, roll out the pasta dough to a thickness of 2mm (1/16 in), and divide the sheet in two. Place one sheet on the floured work surface and dot with tsp of the filling at 2.5cm (1 in) intervals. Place the other sheet on top, and press down gently between the little mounds of filling, making sure the pasta sticks together all around it. Using a serrated pastry wheel, cut into squares, and leave to dry for a while on a floured cloth.

Cook the agnolotti in plenty of salted water for about 6 or 7 minutes. Meanwhile, melt the butter, add the sage leaves and fry briefly. Drain the agnolotti and add to the melted butter. Lightly toss, then sprinkle with some freshly grated Parmesan, and serve.

Serve ten agnolotti per person if you make them about 4cm (1½ in) in size, a few more if they are smaller.

cappellacci with mushroom sauce

6 Once you are adept at making pasta at home, this dish will be easy. Like the previous recipe, it requires a little patience and a fair amount of ambition, but the result will be worth it! The cappellacci can even be made the day before, but they must be stored overnight in the refrigerator wrapped in a clean cloth. 9

serves 6–8 (about 5 cappellacci each)

450g (1 lb) *Basic Pasta Dough* (see page 56)

1 egg, beaten

55g (2 oz) Parmesan, freshly grated

salt and pepper to taste

Filling

150g (5½ oz) fresh Italian sausage, skins removed, or finely minced fresh pork

1 tbsp olive oil

55g (2 oz) roasted shelled hazelnuts, finely chopped

4 tbsp freshly grated Parmesan

2 tbsp each of chopped fresh flat-leaf parsley and chives

5 grates of nutmeg

3–4 tbsp double cream

Make the pasta according to the basic recipe, and set it aside, covered, while you make the filling. Lightly fry the sausage meat or pork for a few minutes in the olive oil, then set aside. When cool, mix with all the other filling ingredients.

Roll out the pasta dough as thinly as possible and cut into circles of 8–9cm (about 3½ in) in diameter. Cut only two to three circles at a time and always leave the pasta sheet covered with a cloth to prevent it from drying. Place a level tsp of the filling on each circle and fold over, sealing the edge with a little beaten egg. Then roll the semi-circle of sealed pasta into a sausage and bend it round to join the ends together, pressing the seal down on the work surface with your thumb.

For the sauce, thoroughly clean both types of fresh mushroom, then cut them into slices and fry in the butter. After they have cooked for a little while, add the garlic and continue to cook for a couple of minutes more. Add the wine, salt and pepper and let the liquid evaporate over a high flame for a minute or two. Then add the parsley. If using field mushrooms, add the drained dried porcini, chopped, with the fresh mushrooms. (Save the soaking water for another dish.)

In the meantime, cook the pasta for about 8 minutes, drain and mix it into the sauce. Sprinkle with the Parmesan and serve.

Sauce

250g (9 oz) fresh ceps, or 250g (9 oz) field mushrooms, plus 25g (1 oz) dried porcini soaked for 10 minutes in warm water

55g (2 oz) butter

1 garlic clove, finely chopped

75ml (2½ fl oz) dry white wine

1 tbsp chopped fresh flat-leaf parsley

Tortelloni di Magro
meatless tortelloni

6 The word "magro" means that the filling is based on vegetables and cheese and does not contain any meat. This is a very light and tasty dish which I recommend to all vegetarians. Accompany it with a fresh wild salad, and you will have a lovely summer meal. If, however, you add a meat sauce, you can make a more substantial main-course dish. 9

serves 4

450g (1 lb) *Basic Pasta Dough* (see page 56)

55g (2 oz) butter, melted

55g (2 oz) Parmesan, freshly grated

salt and pepper to taste

Filling

250g (9 oz) Swiss chard or spinach leaves

150g (5½ oz) fresh ricotta cheese, crumbled

1 tbsp chopped fresh mint or other herbs

4 tbsp freshly grated Parmesan

The essential ingredients are ricotta, which is a very low-fat cheese, and herbs, which can be varied according to their availability. I have made this dish with such herbs as mint, basil, coriander, chives, parsley, and either a little Swiss chard or spinach.

Clean and cook the chard (with its white stalks removed) or spinach leaves, then drain well, squeeze out excess water, and finely chop.

Make the filling by mixing together the chopped chard or spinach, the ricotta, herbs, Parmesan and some salt and pepper.

Prepare the pasta as in the basic recipe and roll it out as thinly as possible. Cut it into squares of about 6cm (2½ in). Place a tsp of the filling in one corner of each square, and fold the opposite corner over to make a triangle. Press the edges together to secure. You may need a little water (or egg white) to ensure the pasta sticks firmly. Now gently fold the two side corners around your finger to meet, making a circular shape. Press to seal.

Cook in plenty of boiling salted water for about 6–7 minutes. Drain and add to it the melted butter, then serve immediately with grated Parmesan.

Ravioli di Gamberoni
prawn ravioli

serves 4

450g (1 lb) *Basic Pasta Dough* (see page 56)

2 tbsp coarsely chopped fresh chives to garnish

salt and pepper to taste

Filling

200g (7 oz) giant prawns

1 tsp chopped fresh chives

4 tbsp freshly grated Parmesan

1 tbsp finely chopped fresh flat-leaf parsley

❛ Although ravioli can be made with almost any kind of fish, the best results are generally obtained with delicately flavoured, firm-fleshed fish. Likewise the accompanying sauce should be neither too rich nor too thick. ❜

Cook the prawns in 200ml (7 fl oz) water, which you should keep for the sauce. When cooked, about 5–6 minutes, peel the prawns and blend the flesh together with the other filling ingredients and some salt and pepper for about 10 seconds, or until they are only roughly puréed.

In the meantime, prepare the pasta dough and roll it out into thin sheets of equal size. Place on the pasta sheets at intervals of about 5cm (2 in) about a ½ tsp filling for each ravioli. Cover with a second layer of pasta dough and proceed to cut out the ravioli shapes (see page 59).

For the sauce, melt the butter in a pan, add the saffron and fry for a few seconds. Add the water, and when this starts to boil, take off the heat and beat in the egg yolks vigorously. Stir over a gentle heat until the sauce starts to thicken, then season with salt and pepper.

Cook the ravioli in boiling salted water for about 7–8 minutes, then drain well. Cover with the sauce, and at the last moment, sprinkle the chives over the top.

Sauce

40g (1½ oz) butter

1 sachet powdered saffron

50ml (2 fl oz) prawn cooking water (see method)

2 large egg yolks

Pappardelle al Sugo di Arrosto
pappardelle with roast beef sauce

serves 4

450g (1 lb) home-made
pappardelle (see page 56), or
400g (14 oz) dried pappardelle

200ml (7 fl oz) roast beef juices
(use stock to augment the meat
juices if necessary)

75ml (2½ fl oz) dry white wine

55g (2 oz) butter

55g (2 oz) Parmesan, freshly
grated

salt and pepper to taste

❝ Pappardelle is a typical Tuscan pasta which is usually served with a sauce based on hare meat, "al sugo di lepre". I find this roast beef sauce even more succulent. The sauce is made simply by heating up the dish in which you have roasted some beef, and dissolving the delicious pan juices in some wine. (The juices from a good roast chicken could be used too, but beef is still the best!) ❞

To make the sauce, scoop away most of the congealed fat from the pan in which you cooked the beef. If the juices are still warm and liquid, remove excess fat by mopping up with absorbent kitchen paper. Heat the dish over a low flame and use a spoon to scrape away and dislodge the tasty residue in the bottom of the pan. As the meat juices begin to bubble, stir in the wine to deglaze the pan. Add a nut of the butter and some salt and pepper if necessary.

Meanwhile, cook the pappardelle until al dente in boiling salted water, then drain and immediately mix with the remaining butter, the freshly grated Parmesan and the seasoned meat juices. Serve in heated pasta bowls as an exceptional first course.

pasta with beans

serves 6

> 6 This is one of the rare pasta dishes that enjoys equal popularity in all the different Italian regions, one of the great classics. The best version is said to come from Naples, where scraps of pasta from the ends of different packets are mixed with spaghetti crushed into spoon-sized pieces. 9

1kg (2¼ lb) fresh borlotti beans, or 250g (9 oz) dried borlotti or cannellini beans, or 2 x 425g (15 oz) cans unsalted borlotti beans

2 celery stalks, finely chopped

115g (4 oz) prosciutto trimmings, chopped into small cubes

4 tbsp extra virgin olive oil

2 medium potatoes, cut into cubes

1 fresh red chilli, chopped

2 garlic cloves, finely chopped

3 ripe tomatoes, skinned and chopped, or 1 x 425g (15 oz) can peeled plum tomatoes, chopped in the can

1 litre (1¾ pints) *Chicken Stock* or *Beef Stock* (see page 40) or water

115g (4 oz) tubettini or mixed pasta

10 fresh basil leaves, shredded

salt and pepper to taste

The best beans to use are fresh borlotti beans, which are occasionally to be found outside Italy now. Available around August and September, they are recognisable by the green and red colouring of the pods. If you can't find fresh, you can use canned, but another alternative is white cannellini beans.

If you are using dried beans, leave them to soak in water the night before you use them. Then boil them in some unsalted water for 2–3 hours until they are tender. If you are using fresh beans boil these for 30–40 minutes until they are cooked. Simply drain and rinse canned beans.

Fry the celery and prosciutto in a large saucepan in the olive oil over a medium heat. After a few minutes add the potatoes and chilli, stirring to prevent the prosciutto from browning. After about 10 minutes add the garlic and cook it for a couple of minutes before adding the tomatoes. Wait a further 10 minutes before adding two-thirds of the drained beans, keeping the remainder aside to be mashed and added to thicken the dish. Pour in the stock or water and bring to the boil. Now add the pasta and, after 8 minutes add the basil leaves and the mashed beans. Season with salt and pepper.

When serving, a trickle of extra virgin olive oil on the top of each dish will enhance the flavour amazingly.

sardinian pasta with sausage and tomato sauce

6 Sardinia has many specialities which are quite different from the rest of Italy. Most dishes are of peasant origin, and they demonstrate how poor people managed to satisfy their dietary needs using only combinations of humble ingredients, but which resulted in wonderful flavours. Sardinian dishes are now enjoying a well-deserved renaissance.9

serves 4

400g (14 oz) Sardinian gnocchetti

salt and pepper to taste

Sauce

6 tbsp olive oil

1 small onion, finely chopped

1 garlic clove, finely chopped

300g (10½ oz) fresh Italian sausage (luganega), meat removed from the casing, crumbled

35g (1¼ oz) dried porcini, soaked for half an hour, then finely chopped (keep the liquid)

3 tbsp dry white wine

600g (1 lb 5 oz) polpa di pomodoro (crushed tomatoes)

Gnocchetti are rather chunky pasta shapes – concave with a ribbed back – made with pure durum wheat semolina, and they take rather longer to cook than normal pasta. They are also known as 'malloreddus'.

For the sauce, heat the oil in a casserole, add the onion, and let it cook for 5 minutes over a moderate heat until softened. Add the garlic and cook for another minute before adding the sausage and porcini. Allow to brown, stirring, then pour in the wine and the tomato pulp. Leave to cook over a very low heat for about an hour. If more moisture is needed, add a little of the mushroom soaking liquid. When ready, season to taste with salt and pepper.

Cook the pasta in plenty of boiling salted water until al dente, about 10–12 minutes.

Mix the pasta with the sauce and serve immediately. If you like, you could add some freshly grated Parmesan or pecorino, but I prefer it without. The sauce, if you leave the sausage in larger chunks, could also be served with polenta.

Spaghettini con Frutti di Mare
seafood spaghettini

6 Seafood pastas are basics of Italian gastronomy, but will vary enormously from region to region: the spaghetti vongole from Naples, the Venetian black spaghetti with cuttlefish, pasta with mussels and limpets from Positano and spaghetti and sea urchins from Puglia. The most important thing to remember is that the seafood must be the very freshest possible. It is the liquid the clams or mussels produce in cooking that contributes enormously to the flavour. 9

serves 4

400g (14 oz) spaghettini

salt and pepper to taste

Sauce

1.8kg (4 lb) mixed fresh shellfish such as clams, mussels etc.

4 tbsp olive oil

2 garlic cloves, thinly sliced

1 dried red chilli

75ml (2½ fl oz) dry white wine

2 tbsp chopped fresh flat-leaf parsley

Clean the shellfish under running water with a small brush. Then put them all into a saucepan containing about 1cm (½ in) water and heat over a high flame. Cover the pan with a lid and shake vigorously a few times until all the shells have opened. Remove from the heat and leave to cool. (Discard any that remain closed.) Take the fish from their shells and carefully strain their cooking liquid. Leave some of the shellfish in their shells to use as a garnish.

Heat the olive oil in a large heavy pan, add the garlic and fry for about a minute, taking care that it does not brown. Crumble the chilli into the garlic and add the wine, letting it evaporate a little. Pour in the shelled fish and their liquid and finally add the parsley.

Cook the spaghettini until al dente, then drain and mix in a little of the sauce. Divide between preheated bowls with the rest of the sauce and lots of black pepper. Garnish with the shells.

pesto sauce

makes 200g (7 oz)
pesto

2 fistfuls fresh basil leaves

1 garlic clove

25g (1 oz) pine nuts

about 125ml (4 fl oz) olive oil

4 tbsp freshly grated pecorino
piccante cheese

4 tbsp freshly grated Parmesan

salt to taste

❝ This recipe requires a fair amount of fresh basil. If you cannot find enough, supplement one fistful with fresh flat-leaf parsley. This alternative makes an excellent, albeit different, pesto. In most countries, it is possible to make a lot of pesto when basil is plentiful and not at an exorbitant price. To preserve it, you should take the quantities in this recipe and multiply them by four. This will give you about sixteen or so individual portions, which are best divided between small jars. ❞

The simplest way to make this sauce is to put all the ingredients in an electric mixer and blend very briefly until you have a rough-textured sauce. You can also pound the ingredients in a pestle and mortar. The latter will have a completely different texture to the former, and I don't mind the extra work. Alternatively, you can chop everything very finely with a sharp knife.

Chop the basil leaves roughly and slice the garlic. In your pestle, grind the garlic to a paste, then add the basil leaves and pound until they begin to break up. Add the pine nuts and, as you pound them, they will begin to amalgamate with the basil. At this point, slowly start to dribble in the olive oil, enough to obtain a semi-liquid sauce. When the sauce has become liquid enough, add the cheeses, stir in well, and season lightly with salt. The amount of salt depends on the type of pecorino used. Some can be very salty.

Pesto can also be frozen (see page 15).

trofie with pesto sauce

serves 4

400g (14 oz) dried trofie or trenette

4 tbsp freshly grated Parmesan

some fresh salad leaves

salt to taste

'Improved pesto sauce'

4 tbsp extra virgin olive oil

1 x 115g (4 oz) jar bought pesto

2 tbsp chopped fresh basil

½ garlic clove, finely chopped

20g (¾ oz) butter

❝ The famous pesto alla genovese is without doubt one of the classic sauce recipes of Italian cooking. Its true home, however, is in Liguria, where the ingredients needed can be obtained all year round. There are many different variations of this sauce, which is always accompanied by the large flat spaghetti called trenette, or else by home-made pasta shapes called trofie. (The latter are now available dried in good delicatessens.) ❞

In summer when basil is in season and abundant, it's worth not only making pesto freshly for this dish according to the recipe on page 69, but making a quantity large enough to freeze. Out of season, however, when you can come by only a couple of fresh basil leaves, I suggest you 'improve' a jar of bought pesto by freshening it up in the following way.

Cook the pasta in boiling salted water until al dente, about 10 minutes.

Meanwhile, make the sauce. Gently heat the olive oil in a small saucepan, and add the pesto from the jar, the basil, garlic and butter. Stir briefly, and then add a little of the pasta cooking water.

Drain the pasta and mix with half the sauce and the grated Parmesan, put the remainder of the sauce on top, then mix well and serve immediately with some fresh leaves.

If you are lucky enough to be using freshly made pesto, gently warm 200g (7 oz) pesto over a low heat, but do not boil. Dilute the sauce with 2 or 3 tbsp of the pasta cooking water, drain the pasta and proceed as above.

Orecchiette Baresi con Pomodorini e Frutti di Mare

little puglian ears with seafood and cherry tomatoes

serves 4

> ❛ The most basic ingredients of Puglian cooking are the "pomodorini" – little sweet, round cherry tomatoes – and olive oil. If you then include a typical pasta – orecchiette, which used to be made by hand – and some seafood from the coastal towns and villages, you only need a couple of glasses of the very good Puglian wine to complete a picture of Mediterranean pleasure! ❜

400g (14 oz) orecchiette (from Bari or Puglia)

salt to taste

The clams and mussels for the sauce can be opened by putting them in a pan with a tbsp of the oil and heating over a low heat until the shells open. Discard any that remain closed. Keep the cooking liquid. Remove the shells from most of the clams, keeping a few in shell for decoration, and from all the mussels and scallops. Trim and clean the scallops and the squid, and cut into serving pieces. Wash and dry the scallops and squid.

Put the remaining oil in a pan and gently fry the garlic and chilli to soften slightly, then add the tomatoes and fry for 5 minutes. Add the squid, the scallops and the parsley, and cook for a further 5 minutes. Add the mussels and clams and their cooking liquid, and warm through only.

Meanwhile, cook the pasta in plenty of boiling salted water for 12–15 minutes. It will still be al dente after all this cooking time!

Drain the pasta well, add to the sauce, and check the seasoning. Serve immediately. You may have to use a spoon to eat this pasta, as it will have quite a lot of sauce.

Sauce

800g (1¾ lb) mixed seafood (clams, mussels, scallops, squid etc.), washed

50ml (2 fl oz) extra virgin olive oil

2 garlic cloves, finely chopped

1 fresh red chilli, not too hot, finely chopped

400g (14 oz) ripe cherry tomatoes (or use preserved from a jar)

a small bunch of fresh flat-leaf parsley, finely chopped

bucatini with bacon and eggs

serves 4

6 Some people say the name "carbonara" is derived from the Carbonari, those revolutionaries who before 1861 worked to unify Italy. Somebody else says carbonara derives from coal or charcoal, perhaps because the Carbonari would hide in coal cellars… Wherever it comes from, whoever cooked it for the first time had a brilliant idea: the use of uncooked egg yolks as a sauce. Use the thickest spaghetti you can find, or bucatini, a thick spaghetti with a hole through it. 9

400g (14 oz) dried bucatini

salt and pepper to taste

Sauce

200g (7 oz) pancetta affumicata in the piece (in Rome they use guanciale, air-dried pig cheek)

2 large eggs and 2 egg yolks (preferably free-range)

55g (2 oz) Parmesan, freshly grated

3 tbsp olive oil

Remove the skin and little bones from the piece of pancetta. Cut into 1cm (½ in) strips, and then into cubes. Beat the egg yolks with the eggs, add a pinch of salt (depending on how salty the pancetta is), some pepper and the grated Parmesan.

Heat the olive oil in a pan and fry the pancetta, turning the pieces over until they become golden and slightly crisp.

Put the bucatini into boiling salted water and cook until al dente, about 8–10 minutes. Drain, using the hot water to warm your serving bowl. Mix the drained bucatini with the pancetta and the hot oil from the pan. Put into your heated serving bowl and mix together with the egg and Parmesan mixture. Season and serve immediately with extra grated Parmesan on the table, and perhaps some more twists of pepper.

Tagliolini Primavera
spring tagliolini

> ❛ Why I persist in calling this dish "spring" tagliolini is a mystery even to me, as most of the herbs involved are to be found throughout the summer months. You can, however, make this recipe as soon as you find sufficient quantities of the fresh herbs which form the basis of the sauce. ❜

serves 4

450g (1 lb) *Basic Pasta Dough* (see page 56), or 400g (14 oz) dried paglia e fieno

salt and pepper to taste

The ideal pasta for this dish is home-made tagliolini, but you could use dried: 'paglia e fieno', 'straw and hay', so called because the thin ribbons are mixed green and yellow, would be suitable.

Make the pasta dough according to the basic recipe. Roll it out and cut it into tagliolini – the thinnest of pasta ribbons.

Make a paste by chopping together on a board all the herbs (include any others that you might have, such as thyme or marjoram) and the pine nuts, and then mix them with the oil in a bowl. In a pan melt the butter, add the garlic, and just allow it to soften.

Cook the pasta in boiling salted water: the dried will take 5 minutes, the fresh 3 minutes. Drain, retaining a little of the cooking water.

At this point, mix the garlic and butter in with the herb paste and the Parmesan, season with salt and pepper, and add a drop of the hot pasta water to make the sauce creamier in consistency. Thoroughly mix the herb paste into the pasta, taste for seasoning, and serve immediately on warm plates.

Sauce

2 tbsp each of chopped fresh mint, coriander, flat-leaf parsley and basil

1 tbsp each of chopped fresh dill and sage

30g (a good 1 oz) pine nuts, chopped

2 tbsp olive oil

115g (4 oz) butter

1 garlic clove, finely chopped

30g (a good 1 oz) Parmesan, freshly grated

black fettuccine with mussels, garlic and parsley

6 Peoci are those beautiful Adriatic mussels, very sweet in taste, that you can find only in the Venetian laguna. And in Venice you will also find the very small tender seppia or cuttlefish, whose ink is the basis of so many wonderful Venetian recipes, and of home-made black pasta.9

serves 4

400g (14 oz) home-made black fettuccine (see right), or dried black fettuccine or tagliatelle

2 tbsp chopped fresh flat-leaf parsley to garnish

salt and pepper to taste

Sauce

1.3kg (3 lb) fresh mussels in their shells

4 tbsp olive oil

1 garlic clove, finely chopped

For home-made black pasta, use 400g (14 oz) flour, 2 medium eggs and the ink from 2 small cuttlefish diluted with enough water to make 100ml (3½ fl oz). Make as the *Basic Pasta Dough* on page 56.

Scrub the mussels clean. In a saucepan with a lid put the mussels and 2 tbsp of the olive oil. Over a strong flame steam the mussels open, shaking the pan every so often. The moment the mussels are all open (discard any that remain closed), put the pan aside to cool a little. When cool remove the mussels from their shells and carefully strain and retain their cooking liquid.

In a separate pan heat the remainder of the olive oil, and fry the garlic for a minute. Add the mussel liquid, and evaporate a little just to reduce the sauce. Add the mussels and remove from the heat.

Cook the fresh fettuccine in plenty of boiling salted water until al dente, which will take less than 1 minute (longer if dried, of course). Drain and add to the mussels in the pan. Stir together for a minute to fully incorporate the flavour of the sauce. Scatter the parsley over and serve immediately.

gourmet lasagne

> 6 This dish reminds me above all of those apparently never-ending Christmas meals where succulent course follows succulent course. As it requires quite a lot of preparation, I suggest that you only make it on really special occasions. Because festoni is so rich and substantial, you may wish to make it a main course, accompanied only by salad. 9

serves 8 as a main course

Meatballs

300g (10½ oz) minced beef

1 garlic clove, finely chopped

1 tbsp chopped fresh flat-leaf parsley

30g (a good 1 oz) Parmesan, freshly grated

2 medium eggs, beaten

40g (1½ oz) fresh breadcrumbs, soaked in a little milk and then squeezed dry

olive oil for frying

salt and pepper to taste

The word 'festoni' is the equivalent of the English word 'festoon', and that is what the pasta looks like. It is similar to pappardelle, a ribbon of up to 2.5cm (I in) wide, which is frilled along one or both sides.

For the meatballs, make a paste by mixing the minced beef, the garlic, parsley, Parmesan, eggs and soaked breadcrumbs together. When you have thoroughly stirred this mixture and added some salt and pepper, start shaping it into little walnut-sized meatballs. Fry these in some oil until they are golden.

Prepare the sauce by frying the onion in the oil. When it is only half cooked, add the chopped chicken livers. After about 3 minutes' frying, add the tomatoes and continue to simmer for about half an hour over a low heat. Towards the end of this time, add the fresh basil leaves and some salt and pepper.

Preheat the oven to 200°C/400°F/Gas 6.

Cook the pasta for 5–7 minutes in boiling salted water or until it is very al dente, drain, then add some of the tomato sauce so that it is all coated.

Take a deep baking tin and start layering the festoni by spreading some tomato sauce over the bottom. On this arrange some of the cooked pasta. Next on top of the pasta place some

Tomato sauce

1 medium onion, chopped

4 tbsp olive oil

115g (4 oz) chicken livers, washed, dried and chopped

2 x 800g (1¾ lb) cans peeled plum tomatoes, chopped in the cans, or polpa di pomodoro

10 basil leaves, torn

Layers

500g (1 lb 2 oz) festoni pasta

115g (4 oz) spicy Neapolitan salami, thinly sliced

300g (10½ oz) fontina or taleggio cheese, sliced

85g (3 oz) Parmesan, freshly grated

4 medium eggs, beaten

of the sliced salami, some meatballs and some slices of fontina or taleggio. Cover these with another 3–4 tbsp sauce and a sprinkling of Parmesan. Repeat this procedure until you have used up all the ingredients other than the sauce and Parmesan. When you have reached the final layer of cheese, pour on the well-beaten eggs, which will bind the pasta together. Over this pour the last of the sauce and the remaining Parmesan.

Put the tin into the preheated oven for 25 minutes. When ready, golden and sizzling, leave the dish for 5 minutes before dividing into portions with a knife, and serving hot.

basic gnocchi

> ❝ The official translation of the word "gnocchi" in English should be "dumplings". But, unlike their English counterparts, which are a suet-based accompaniment to stews, gnocchi are much lighter and are eaten as a first-course dish with various sauces, ranging from simple tomato to walnut or Gorgonzola. ❞

serves 4–6

900g (2 lb) floury potatoes

200g (7 oz) plain flour, plus extra for dusting

salt and pepper to taste

To serve

freshly grated Parmesan

butter

Other varieties of gnocchi can be made with semolina, ricotta, chickpea flour or even chestnut flour.

Peel the potatoes and boil them in a little water in a closed saucepan until they are completely cooked. Drain away the remaining water very carefully, and thoroughly mash the potatoes while they are still warm – don't leave any lumps. Then start to knead the mash on a floured work surface, adding flour from time to time, so that you obtain a soft but elastic dough. Add salt and pepper to taste.

Next, take a piece of the dough, sprinkle it with some extra flour, and roll it with your hands into a sausage-like shape 2cm (¾ in) in diameter. Slice this cylinder of dough into little pieces 3cm (1¼in) long. Repeat this operation until all the dough has been cut into chunks. Then take a large, preferably wooden fork, and hold it in your left hand, prongs down. With your thumb squeeze each chunk of dough against the prongs, letting the gnocchi roll off on to a clean cloth. Repeat with all the chunks. They should curl up like ribbed shells.

Cook the gnocchi in abundant salted boiling water. When they are ready you will see them float to the surface, a few minutes only. Scoop them out using a slotted spoon to drain all the water away, and place directly in a preheated dish. Sprinkle with a little freshly grated Parmesan and pieces of butter.

Strangulaprievete
priest-choker

> ❝ The strange name given to this dish is attributed to the commonly known fact that a good Italian priest loves good food. Indeed, one such Neapolitan priest is said to have loved gnocchi so much that he choked when he ate too much too fast! There are a variety of different recipes bearing this name throughout the Italian regions, some for potato gnocchi, some for pasta, and in the north, for bread dumplings. ❞

serves 6

1 recipe *Basic Gnocchi* (see opposite)

55g (2 oz) Parmesan, freshly grated

salt and pepper to taste

Make the sauce by pouring the tomatoes into the heated olive oil. Simmer for 15 minutes, stirring from time to time, until the sauce has begun to thicken, then add the basil leaves and some salt and pepper to taste.

Now cook the gnocchi as described in the previous recipe, drain well and put in a heated dish. Add the Parmesan and the sauce, and mix thoroughly into the gnocchi. Serve hot – and be careful not to choke!

Sauce

1 x 800g (1¾ lb) can peeled plum tomatoes, chopped in the can

3 tbsp olive oil

10 basil leaves, torn

spinach gnocchi with gorgonzola sauce

> The essence of gnocchi is their lightness. Make sure the spinach is really well drained, and use the right proportions of ingredients. In season you can use wild stinging nettles in the same way as spinach. They give the gnocchi a particularly good and nutty flavour.

serves 4

750g (1 lb 10 oz) floury potatoes (peeled weight)

200g (7 oz) spinach, tough stalks removed

200g (7 oz) plain flour

1 large egg, beaten

salt and pepper to taste

Sauce

115g (4 oz) Gorgonzola cheese

150ml (5 fl oz) milk

55g (2 oz) butter

To serve

55g (2 oz) Parmesan, freshly grated

For the sauce, cut the Gorgonzola into cubes and soak in the milk for half an hour while you make the gnocchi.

Cook the potatoes until soft, and pass them through a food mill. Wash the spinach thoroughly and cook it in a very little water. Drain, carefully squeeze out all excess water, then chop finely. Add the spinach to the potatoes with the flour, beaten egg and seasonings, and mix well together. Shape and cook the gnocchi as in the basic recipe on page 80.

Continue the sauce by melting the butter in a saucepan, then add the Gorgonzola and milk. Stir until the ingredients have amalgamated. When the gnocchi are cooked, add them to the sauce, add the grated Parmesan, mix well and serve hot.

Gnocchi alla Romana
semolina gnocchi

serves 4

1 litre (1¾ pints) milk

½ tsp salt

4 grates of nutmeg

450g (1 lb) coarse semolina flour

2 eggs plus 1 egg yolk, beaten

55g (2 oz) butter

30g (a good 1 oz) Parmesan, freshly grated

❝ This speciality from the Lazio region does not bear much resemblance to the gnocchi dishes described above, as the basic mixture is made differently, using semolina flour and milk. Serve either as a first course or as a side dish for a stew. ❞

A Sicilian version of this uses chickpea flour instead of semolina. The result is similar to 'panelle', the speciality of Palermo, which is cooked flat like a frittata, and then put between slices of toasted bread as a sandwich.

Heat the milk together with the salt and nutmeg. When it begins to boil add the semolina flour little by little, stirring all the time with a whisk so that lumps do not form. Once all the semolina is incorporated, leave the mixture to simmer for about 20 minutes over a low heat, stirring from time to time.

Next take the pan from the stove, leave it a moment or so to cool down, then thoroughly stir in the beaten egg. Pour the mixture out on to a working surface (this should preferably be marble but if it is wood take care to slightly dampen the surface beforehand). Using some kind of spatula, evenly spread the warm mixture to a thickness of 2cm (¾ in). Let it cool down.

In the meantime, grease a baking tin or dish with some butter, and preheat the oven to 220°C/425°F/Gas 7.

Using a glass or a pastry cutter 5cm (2 in) in diameter, cut out discs from the semolina pasta and then place them in the tin, one overlapping the other. Dot the gnocchi with little pieces of butter and place in the preheated oven until the tips of the gnocchi begin to brown, about 15 minutes. Take the dish out of the oven, sprinkle with the Parmesan, and serve immediately.

basic pizza

6 There are so many different combinations of ingredients that it is hard for me to give a global definition of pizza. If pressed, however, I would say that it is a species of flat bread, which (as its cooking time is very short) can be topped by anything that takes your fancy. The pizza has become so famed worldwide that even foreigners are now making and inventing their own variations, often adding the most unusual ingredients to the topping. 9

makes 4 x 28cm (11 in) pizzas

35g (1¼ oz) fresh yeast (or the equivalent quantity of dried yeast: see maker's instructions)

300ml (10 fl oz) warm water

a pinch of salt

2 tbsp olive oil, plus extra for greasing

600g (1 lb 5 oz) '00' flour, plus extra for dusting

Dissolve the yeast in the warm water to which you have added the salt and olive oil. Leave to froth, about 10 minutes. Pour the flour into a mound on a clean work surface and make a hole in the centre of it. Add the yeast mixture drop by drop into the centre of the flour, mixing with your hands until all the liquid is absorbed, forming large lumps. Knead the dough with your hands until it has a smooth texture, then roll it into a ball. A good pizza depends on the quality of the dough used.

Next, sprinkle some extra flour into a large bowl, and place the dough in it, spreading a little oil over the top to prevent a crust from forming. Cover the bowl with a dry linen cloth and leave to rise for an hour in a warm place – not less than 20°C/68°F. (It was at this stage that my grandmother used to 'bless' the dough by making the sign of the cross in order that it should turn out well.) After this time the dough should have increased in volume by about three times.

Now begins the preparation of the pizza proper. Preheat the oven to 230°C/450°F/Gas 8. Rub four 28cm (11 in) pizza pans or a couple of large baking trays with olive oil. Flour the work surface. Divide the dough into four and roll each into a ball. (It is better not to use a rolling pin, but to ease the dough by gently pressing out the dough with the plump part of your hand, the heel of your thumb and with your fingers.) Starting from the middle, smooth the dough out to a thickness of about 5mm (¼ in). Make the edges slightly thicker to prevent the topping from running off, which leaves the characteristic round edge which should go crisp in the oven.

Place each pizza on an oiled pizza pan or on the trays, spread the chosen topping on the pizza and bake in the preheated oven for anything from 8–15 minutes, depending on the ingredients. See times specified for each individual recipe.

Pizza alla Napoletana
(see page 86).

Pizza alla Napoletana
neapolitan pizza

makes 4 x 28cm
(11 in) pizzas

Basic Pizza Dough made with
600g (1 lb 5 oz) '00' flour
(see page 84)

extra virgin olive oil

Sauce and topping

2 tbsp olive oil

1 garlic clove, chopped

12 ripe plum tomatoes, skinned
and halved, or 1 x 800g (1¾ lb)
can peeled plum tomatoes,
chopped in the can, or polpa di
pomodoro

2 tsp dried oregano

salt and pepper to taste

❝ This classic pizza is both one of the simplest to prepare and the most tasty. In Naples it is customary to eat pizza in one's hands. ❞

Prepare the dough as described in the basic recipe. Make the tomato sauce while the dough is rising. Preheat the oven to 230°C/450°F/Gas 8.

For the sauce, heat the oil in a pan, fry the garlic for just a few seconds and then add the tomatoes (if using canned tomatoes you may have to strain out some of the extra liquid). Simmer the sauce, stirring from time to time, for 15 minutes. Season with salt and pepper.

Grease each pizza pan or baking tray with a brush dipped in oil. Divide the dough into four and form into pizzas as described on page 85. Place the dough circles in the pans or on the trays and smooth them out so that they fit perfectly and are of a uniform thickness. Spread on each circle of dough 2 spoonfuls of the tomato sauce. Sprinkle this with the oregano. Pour a tbsp of olive oil over the top of each and place in the preheated oven for about 10–15 minutes, until you see the edges become a golden brown colour. (See the photograph on page 85.)

Pizza Margherita
tomato and cheese pizza

makes 4 x 28cm (11 in) pizzas

Basic Pizza Dough made with 600g (1 lb 5 oz) '00' flour (see page 84)

extra virgin olive oil

Sauce

2 tbsp olive oil

2 garlic cloves, finely chopped

12 ripe plum tomatoes, skinned and halved, or 1 x 800g (1¾ lb) can peeled plum tomatoes, chopped in the can, or polpa di pomodoro

salt and pepper to taste

6 I've published this pizza a couple of times, but it is an absolute classic – and is as easy to prepare as the one opposite, simply with the addition of mozzarella cheese. It was reputed to have been created to honour Queen Margherita of Italy. In fact its colouring is rather Italian, the red of the tomatoes, the white of the mozzarella and the green of the basil echoing the colours of the Italian flag. 9

Make the basic dough as described on page 84, and leave it to rise. Then follow the instructions for *Neapolitan Pizza* on the page opposite, making a tomato sauce, until you come to the final topping. Preheat the oven to 230°C/450°F/Gas 8.

Grease the pizza pans or baking trays, and form the risen dough into four pizzas. Chop the mozzarella into small cubes, and scatter them over the dough which you have spread with the tomato sauce. Add the basil leaves, dribble 1 tbsp olive oil all over each pizza, and season with salt and pepper. Bake in the preheated oven for 10–15 minutes.

Topping

200g (7 oz) mozzarella cheese

12 fresh basil leaves

Calzone Imbottito
stuffed pizza

makes 4 calzone

Basic Pizza Dough made with 600g (1 lb 5 oz) '00' flour (see page 84)

a little milk for glazing

olive oil

Filling

115g (4 oz) mozzarella cheese

115g (4 oz) cooked ham

2 eggs

2 tbsp freshly grated Parmesan

4 fresh basil leaves, chopped

200g (7 oz) ricotta cheese

salt and pepper to taste

6 Because the calzone is a kind of "inside-out" pizza, it is able to keep intact all the flavours contained in the filling. This is a slightly heavier recipe than the other pizzas. It can also be made with a variety of different ingredients such as salami, cheese or vegetables. 9

The calzone that my mother used to cook was based on fontina cheese, ham, sausages and eggs. The more classic calzone, however, contains mozzarella. You can make a vegetarian calzone by using ricotta cheese, spinach, egg and Parmesan, or any leftover or roasted vegetables.

Make the dough as described on page 84, and leave to rise. Preheat the oven to 220°C/425°F/Gas 7.

Prepare the filling by cutting the mozzarella and ham into strips. Beat the eggs (keeping a little aside for sealing the dough envelopes), and add the Parmesan, basil, a pinch of salt and a few grinds of black pepper. Mix this in with the ricotta, mozzarella and ham so as to form a reasonably soft paste.

Divide the risen dough into four balls. Flatten these one at a time to form pizzas 1cm (½ in) thick. Next place them on a dry cloth, and put a quarter of the filling on half of each pizza. Cover the filling by folding the pizza in half – use the cloth to help you do this – and seal it by wetting the edge with a little beaten egg and pressing a fork on the join. Brush the dough over with a little milk – this will turn the calzone golden brown when cooked. Place the calzone on a well oiled baking tray and place in the preheated oven for about 15 minutes.

Calzoncini Fritti
little fried calzone

> 6 These stuffed pizzas are wonderful for parties and picnics as all the goodies are enclosed. Children love them. They are equally delicious hot or cold. If you make them to eat as a main course, serve with a tomato sauce. 9

makes 24 calzoncini

Basic Pizza Dough made with 600g (1 lb 5 oz) '00' flour (see page 84)

1 egg, beaten

olive oil

Filling

200g (7 oz) pancetta or smoked bacon

400g (14 oz) ricotta cheese

4 eggs

55g (2 oz) Parmesan, freshly grated

4 tbsp chopped fresh flat-leaf parsley

6 grates of nutmeg

salt and pepper to taste

Make the dough as described on page 84, and leave to rise for an hour.

Cut the pancetta or bacon into matchsticks and fry in 1 tbsp olive oil for a few minutes until golden and slightly crisp. Beat the ricotta together with the eggs, then add the fried pancetta or bacon, Parmesan and parsley. Stir the mixture well, then season with salt, pepper and nutmeg.

Divide the dough into 24 equal pieces. Flour your work surface and roll each piece into little balls and then press out into little circular pizzas measuring 10cm (4 in) in diameter. Place 1 tbsp of the ricotta mixture on one-half of the pizza and fold over to form a half-moon. Seal the join with beaten egg.

When you have made all your little calzoncini, heat 1cm (½ in) olive oil in your pan. When the oil is hot, place the calzoncini in the oil to fry two or three at a time, according to the size of your pan. The oil should not smoke, but be hot enough to turn the calzoncini gently golden as they cook. They will take about 3 minutes on each side. Drain on kitchen paper and serve warm or cold.

Pizza Fritta
fried pizza

makes 8 small pizzas

Basic Pizza Dough made with 600g (1 lb 5 oz) '00' flour (see page 84)

olive oil for deep-frying

150g (5½ oz) Parmesan, freshly grated

> This is a simple pizza that my mother often used to make in order to feed the six ravenous mouths of myself and my brothers.

You will probably need slightly more dedication to make this pizza. It has to be eaten as soon as it is cooked, in order to savour in full its crusty texture. This is such a tasty dish that you will unfortunately be kept working as your guests ask for second helpings. Don't worry if the dough seems to be swimming around in the oil while it is frying, as it will hardly absorb any at all.

Make the basic dough as described on page 84, leave it to rise, and then divide it into eight balls.

For the sauce, fry the garlic in the olive oil until it turns a light golden brown. Then immediately add the tomatoes, basil and some salt, and cook together for 10 minutes.

Heat about 1cm (½ in) of oil until slightly smoking. Flatten out the dough balls until they are about 2.5cm (1 in) thick and then fry them (taking good care not to burn yourself when you turn them) until they become a dark golden brown and are fully cooked inside.

Extract the pizzas from the pan with a fork and put them on a plate, after having shaken off any excess oil. Place a couple of spoonfuls of the sauce on top and sprinkle with a generous amount of grated Parmesan before serving immediately.

Sauce

2 garlic cloves, sliced

6 tbsp olive oil

1 x 800g (1¾ lb) can peeled plum tomatoes, chopped in the can

5 or 6 fresh basil leaves, torn

salt to taste

pizza bread with rosemary

> Focaccia has become almost commonplace throughout Europe, where once it was unfamiliar to all except Italians. This hasn't diminished its deliciousness, though, and home-made focaccia is the best of all. The most common variety is simply topped with some oil and sea salt, and comes in large rectangular shapes which are then cut into squares. It can also be made, however, in the shape of a pizza. Focaccia dough should be slightly thicker than a normal pizza as it is very similar to bread in consistency and, like bread, it can accompany all sorts of foods. "

serves 8–10

85g (3 oz) fresh yeast (or the equivalent amount of dried yeast: see maker's instructions)

600ml (1 pint) warm water

4 tbsp olive oil, plus extra for greasing

1kg (2¼ lb) '00' flour, plus extra for dusting

2 tsp soft brown sugar

Prepare the dough as described on page 84, using the alternative quantities and the sugar instead of salt. Leave it to rise, and preheat the oven to 230°C/450°F/Gas 8.

Roll the dough out until it is either a rectangle or a circle 2.5cm (1 in) thick: this amount of dough makes one big rectangular pizza about 35 x 50cm (14 x 20 in). Place it on an oiled baking tray, cover with a clean cloth and leave to rise again for another hour.

Push down on the dough all over with your fingers to make deep holes, then dribble with 4 tbsp olive oil and scatter with the rosemary leaves. Generously grind fresh pepper and finally sprinkle coarse salt over the whole surface. Bake in the preheated oven for 20 minutes: the top should be golden, but the rosemary must not brown.

To obtain a wonderfully crusty focaccia, pour some extra virgin olive oil on top as it emerges from the oven.

Topping

olive oil

3 tbsp fresh rosemary leaves

coarse salt and black pepper to taste

Grissini
breadsticks

**makes about
20 grissini**

500g (1 lb 2 oz) '00' flour

30g (1¼ oz) fresh bread yeast (or the equivalent dried), dissolved in 75ml (2½ fl oz) warm water

125ml (4 fl oz) extra virgin olive oil

100g (3½ oz) coarse polenta flour or semolina

salt and pepper to taste

❝ This long-lasting bread was created in Turin, in Piedmont, many years ago. They still make them there by hand, stretching the dough to a length of 60–70cm (24–28 in). Many different types of grissini exist, their main function being to replace bread whilst eating antipasti. You can find them flavoured with olives, onions, pepper or just plain. In my opinion the commercially produced grissini you find in most restaurants or delicatessens are inferior to the home made. ❞

'Taralli' are a Puglian speciality, based on the same principle as grissini, but flavoured with olive oil, fennel seeds and black pepper, and curled into a circle before baking.

Mix the plain flour well in a bowl with the yeast and its liquid, the olive oil and salt and pepper to taste. Set aside to rise in a warm place for an hour.

Take a little dough at a time and roll on a dry work surface to make a long, stick-like shape. Roll with both your hands backwards and forwards, at the same time pulling the dough out, so that the stick is 1cm (½ in) in diameter, and at least 25cm (10 in) long. Roll in the polenta flour or semolina, then place on an oiled baking tray. Arrange further grissini on the tray, 1cm (½ in) apart. Cover with a cloth and leave to rise for another 30 minutes.

Meanwhile, preheat the oven to 190°C/375°F/Gas 5.

Bake in the preheated oven until the grissini are pale brown in colour, about 30 minutes. Leave to cool, when they will be dry, crisp and very crunchy.

Pane Casereccio o Rustico
home-style bread

> The direct translation of this would be home-style or rustic bread. Its origins are in Puglia, Calabria and Campania, where the wives would prepare something wholesome, often using leftovers, to give to their farmer husbands when they came home after working on the land. The lard imparts a very special taste, but you can use olive oil instead.

serves 6-8

700g (1 lb 9 oz) '00' flour

40g (1½ oz) fresh bread yeast (or the equivalent dried), dissolved in 75ml (2½ fl oz) warm water

5 medium eggs, beaten, plus 1 extra, also beaten, to glaze

150g (5½ oz) lard, melted, or 150ml (5 fl oz) extra virgin olive oil

1 tsp salt

plenty of freshly ground black pepper

85g (3 oz) provolone cheese, coarsely grated

125g (4½ oz) smoked mozzarella cheese, coarsely grated

100g (3½ oz) pecorino cheese, coarsely grated

55g (2 oz) Parmesan, freshly grated

100g (3½ oz) Neapolitan hot sausage, cut into cubes

55g (2 oz) pancetta, cut into cubes

Put the flour in a large bowl, and add the dissolved yeast liquid, the 5 beaten eggs and the melted lard or olive oil. Mix well to obtain a smooth, not too firm dough. Add the salt, plenty of black pepper, and all the cheeses and meats. Mix very well, and set aside to rise, covered with a cloth, in a warm place.

After 1 hour take out the dough and shape on an oiled baking tray into a large ring. Brush with the remaining beaten egg and leave to rise for another 30 minutes.

Meanwhile, preheat the oven to 190°C/375°F/Gas 5.

Bake in the preheated oven for 35–40 minutes. Remove from the oven and let it cool a little (it is good both hot or cold). Eat accompanied by a very good red wine.

Il Secondo
the main course

There will be a decent interval after il primo is finished before il secondo is served. This is usually meat, poultry, game or fish accompanied by one or two lightly cooked seasonal vegetables or a small salad.

Fish from the Mediterranean is famous for its intense flavour, but sadly, because fish is so popular and is considered a healthy food, the waters around Italy are now in danger of being *over*-fished. There are also many freshwater fish in Italy, and fish farms have recently come into operation. Fish is eaten on a regular basis in Italy, particularly on Friday, because of the strictures of the Catholic religion. I prefer fish cooked simply and accompanied by a flavourful sauce or salsa.

Italian poultry can be excellent, particularly the 'ruspanti', which are completely free-range, living their lives scratching the soil for food. Most Italian chickens are fed with the yellow corn we know as polenta, which gives them a wonderful flavour and colour. Chickens are most often roasted and grilled, and the way of cooking poultry breasts is one that is uniquely Italian. Italy is very fond of 'carne bianca', white meat, into which classification most poultry and some game, like rabbit, fall. There is a great variety of game to choose from – anything that can be shot is shot, including pigeons, partridges, guinea fowl, quail, deer, pheasants and hare. (I must confess to having enjoyed a sparrow once, although I never repeated the experience.) Seasons and hunting areas have been very precisely defined in recent years, in order to allow stock to regenerate. There are many interesting recipes for cooking game – roasts, grills and plenty of hearty stews.

Italy has never been a great meat-eating nation, and relatively few animals are bred for food. The meat that is produced, however, is usually of very good quality. One famous example is the beef grown in the Val

Opposite: *Nodino al Vino* (see page 128).

di Chiana; it is sold as huge, tender T-bone steaks, which are known as 'bistecca alla fiorentina', and are grilled over wood or charcoal fires. (Sadly, because of BSE, a funeral has taken place in Tuscany, the birthplace of la fiorentina, where this piece of beef has been put to rest, at least for the time being.) Veal is considered a meat for those with delicate stomachs and for convalescents. The north – Piedmont, Lombardy and Tuscany – are the regions where both meats are most frequently cooked. Lamb is produced mainly in southern Italy, and has a remarkably delicate flavour. As a result, most of the country's pecorino production is based in the south as well. Very special is the 'abbacchio' of Roman cuisine, which is a young lamb, extremely tender and simply roasted. Lamb is excellent grilled, roasted and made into stews. I like to cook it with vegetables such as artichokes and chicory. Some lamb is produced in the north as well, where the abundant green pasture of the Alps makes for very flavourful lamb and goat meat.

Starting with salami and ham, there are an infinite number of recipes using different pork products – the Italians consider every single part of the pig edible. And there are distinctive regional tastes in pork meat. In Naples, for example, you hear street sellers calling 'O musso', which is boiled pig's nose served with lemon. In the north the pig shin is considered a luxury, while in Tuscany the local roast is the famous 'arista al forno', loin of pork roasted with lots of herbs. And we must include, of course, 'porchetta', which is an entire piglet, boned, stuffed and roasted.

In general, Italians love offal of any kind, from poultry, rabbit, pig, veal, beef and lamb. It belongs to what Italians call 'la cucina povera', the cuisine of the poor, because of the relatively low cost of most offal ingredients.

grilled swordfish 'muddica'

6 The swordfish belongs to the family of large fish which, like tuna, is sold only in slices or steaks. After cooking, and especially if it is fresh, the meat will retain a subtle flavour. Some people compare the texture and taste to veal. When I introduced this recipe to my Carluccio Caffès it became an instant bestseller. It would be best to use a charcoal grill, but gas or electric will do. 9

serves 4

4 swordfish steaks weighing about 200g (7 oz) each, and about 1cm (½ in) thick

8 tbsp very fine fresh breadcrumbs

2 tbsp very finely chopped fresh flat-leaf parsley

1 garlic clove, crushed

olive oil

salt and pepper to taste

Swordfish may be cooked in a variety of different ways, such as grilled or fried. Here is the way the Sicilians do it, using breadcrumbs to carry the flavours. 'Muddica' is the Sicilian pronunciation of 'mollica', which means fresh breadcrumbs. In Sicily they also use this flavourful combination on pasta and other dishes to replace Parmesan.

Mix together the breadcrumbs, parsley and garlic, and season to taste with salt and pepper. Brush the slices of swordfish with olive oil, and then coat both sides with the breadcrumb mixture.

Preheat the grill and cook the fish for 3–4 minutes on each side, depending on the thickness of the fish. The breadcrumbs should be brown and crisp. Serve immediately with lemon wedges and a green salad.

mixed fried fish

6 One of the first dishes that I order whenever I set foot in an Italian seaside town is the fritto misto di pesce. I am sure that everyone who has visited Italy at one time or another will have tried this speciality, which combines the most tender and delicate Mediterranean fish, and includes shellfish, small sole, squid and any number of other fresh and tender creatures from the sea. This dish can be found almost anywhere on the coast of Italy, so any combination of ingredients may be used. 9

serves 4

250g (9 oz) peeled prawns

250g (9 oz) whitebait

250g (9 oz) squid

plenty of plain flour for dusting

olive oil for deep-frying

2 lemons to garnish

salt and pepper to taste

Shell the prawns if necessary. Wash the whitebait and leave to drain and dry. Clean the squid and cut the body into rings. If the squid are small, leave the tentacles whole in their bunches; if they are large, cut them in smaller pieces.

Thoroughly toss all the fish in plenty of flour, shaking off any excess. Heat the olive oil in a deep-fryer or a large saucepan, and immerse the fish in it a few at a time. Cook until they have turned golden in colour, drain carefully on kitchen paper and arrange on a large serving dish. Sprinkle with salt and pepper, and decorate with pieces of lemon.

A good rocket salad will be a clean and delicious accompaniment.

baked anchovies with oregano

6 This is a typical dish from Naples where it is called either "tortiera" or "alici al gratin". It is simplicity itself, provided you can get hold of fresh anchovies. In Italy they are sold in markets like Pozzuoli or Salerno, and even from street vendors on tricycles with large baskets full of fish. If you can't find them, I have had some success with frozen anchovies (or small sardines will do). 9

serves 4

800g (1¾ lb) fresh anchovies (or sardines)

3 tbsp olive oil

2 garlic cloves, finely chopped

1 tsp dried oregano

juice of 1 lemon

2 tbsp dried breadcrumbs

salt to taste

Preheat the oven to 200°C/400°F/Gas 6.

Clean and fillet the anchovies. To do this, cut off the head and tail, open the fish along the stomach, and flatten it gently. Equally gently, pull out the backbone with your thumb and finger. You will find you have two fillets joined together by the skin of the back.

Grease a flat baking tray with a little of the olive oil. Lay on it the anchovies skin side down, as close as possible to one another, but not overlapping. Scatter the garlic and oregano over the anchovies, sprinkle with the lemon juice, then cover with a light layer of the breadcrumbs. Trickle the remainder of the olive oil over the breadcrumbs, season with salt, and place the tray in the oven for 7–8 minutes. Once the breadcrumbs are golden and crisp, the fish will be ready. Unfortunately, they are very difficult to handle, and break up easily (as they did in the photograph!). Serve immediately with some good bread or as bruschetta, accompanied by some salad leaves.

turbot with a piquant sauce

serves 4

6 Turbot is one of the most delicate and sought-after fish, which is also usually big enough to be cut into slices. Whether it is roasted, poached or stewed, turbot still keeps its immaculate white colour and delicate taste. Turbot should always be eaten with boiled potatoes. 9

8 slices of turbot weighing about 100g (3½oz) each

lemon wedges to serve

salt and pepper to taste

Court-bouillon

1.7 litres (3 pints) water

1 small onion, halved

1 carrot, thinly sliced

1 celery stalk, with leaves

1 tsp black peppercorns

2–3 bay leaves

Bring the court-bouillon ingredients to the boil together. When boiling furiously, turn the heat right down, add the slices of turbot and cook very, very gently for from 5–8 minutes, depending on the thickness of the fish.

To make the sauce, melt the butter without burning it. Mix with the remaining sauce ingredients, and season to taste with salt and pepper.

Place the slices of turbot on individual hot plates, and pour the sauce over them. Serve with boiled new potatoes, lemon wedges, and a salad of lamb's lettuce simply dressed with olive oil and lemon juice.

Sauce

85g (3 oz) butter

1 tbsp finely chopped fresh flat-leaf parsley

finely grated rind and juice of 1 lemon

1 tbsp capers, finely chopped

1 small fresh red chilli, very finely chopped

Calamari Fritti
fried squid

serves 4

1kg (2¼ lb) squid, to make about 750g (1 lb 10 oz) when cleaned

a generous quantity of olive oil for deep-frying

plain flour for dusting

2 lemons

salt and pepper to taste

6 Even though this dish is sometimes described as "alla romana", it is common throughout Italy. For this recipe try and find the longer type of squid, as this will have more effect when it is cut into rings. It is cooked more or less in the same way as the fritto misto. In the town of Camogli, near Genoa, a curious annual celebration takes place when local fishermen organise a fried fish festival. To satisfy the thousands of visitors who flock to the town on this occasion, the fishermen install in the marketplace huge frying pans that are 10 metres in diameter. Several hundred litres of oil are used to fry something like 1,000kg or more of fish. The whole meal is totally free and, what is more, accompanied by some excellent wine. 9

To clean the squid, first of all pull the heads and tentacles away from the tubular bodies. The bodies should then be stripped of the outer skin and of the internal transparent 'bone'. Cut away the head but keep the tentacles, which will also be fried. Cut the body into rings; cut the bunches of legs only if they are very long.

Heat the oil in a deep-fryer or a high-sided saucepan. Flour all the pieces of squid well and deep-fry, a large spoonful at a time, so that they don't stick together while cooking. Fry for only 3 or 4 minutes. Drain carefully on kitchen paper, sprinkle with salt and pepper, and serve immediately with slices of lemon and a simple lettuce salad.

Gamberoni all'Aglio, Olio e Peperoncino

prawns in garlic, oil and chilli sauce

serves 4

20–24 large whole raw prawns, peeled, leaving the tail and head attached

12 tbsp olive oil

2 dried red chillies, crumbled

4 garlic cloves, finely chopped

1 tbsp coarsely chopped fresh flat-leaf parsley

❝ These prawns are especially delicious if you take the trouble to peel the body, leaving the flesh exposed so that it can absorb the other flavours. The juices from the head also contribute to the final taste of the sauce. Add chilli to taste – I like it hot! ❞

Try and get some of those famous red and fleshy prawns, sold as gamberoni in Italy. Dublin Bay prawns, French langoustines or Italian scampi may be used instead. An ideal wine to accompany this dish is a good young red, served chilled.

Heat the olive oil in a pan, add the chillies and then immediately the prawns. Fry, turning the prawns over frequently, for 2 minutes. Now add the garlic and parsley and allow the flavours to seep into the prawns – this will take only a few seconds. Don't let the garlic brown. Serve the prawns in warmed individual bowls. Accompany them with some good bread to dip into the flavoured oil. I like to eat the prawns with my hands, and a lot of finger sucking goes on!

Insalata di Baccalà
salt cod salad

> ❝ The large merluzzo or cod is certainly not a typically Italian fish, as it comes mainly from northern seas. However (perhaps following the example of the Spaniards and Portuguese), the Italians have now fully adopted it in the form of baccalà, or salt cod. Indeed, each region has created its own baccalà speciality. The obvious convenience of salt cod is that it keeps, and therefore may be cooked at any season. Care needs to be taken when buying this fish to ensure that it is both thick and white – two qualities that indicate goodness. ❞

serves 4–6

500g (1 lb 2 oz) salt cod: soaked weight 1kg (2¼ lb)

125ml (4 fl oz) extra virgin olive oil

100g (3½ oz) small black Ligurian olives

2 tbsp finely chopped fresh flat-leaf parsley

2 garlic cloves, sliced

juice of 1 lemon

2–3 lemons, halved

freshly ground black pepper to taste

The soaking process (which de-salts the fish) should begin at least 24 hours before the preparation of the dish starts, and the water should be changed three or four times. Try and place the pieces of cod in the water with the skin facing upwards, as you will find that the salt is expelled more rapidly this way. In Italy it is possible to buy salt cod that has already been softened and de-salted by soaking, though in other countries, with the exception of Spain and France, I have been able to find it only in the dried form.

Cover the soaked pieces of salt cod in plenty of fresh water, skin side up. Bring to the boil, then simmer until you see that the skin is beginning to come away from the flesh (at least 30–40 minutes, depending on thickness). Drain and remove all the skin and bones, and any tough bits. Flake the fish coarsely, then dress with the oil, olives, parsley, garlic and lemon juice. Mix well together, and serve with black pepper and lemon.

Baccalà in Umido
salt cod in tomatoes

serves 4

500g (1 lb 2 oz) salt cod: soaked weight 1kg (2¼ lb)

4 tbsp olive oil

2 garlic cloves, chopped

1 x 800g (1¾ lb) can peeled plum tomatoes, chopped in the can

8 basil leaves, torn

salt and pepper to taste

❛ Braising salt cod with tomatoes is common to many regions of Italy. Some people cook potatoes in with the fish: I prefer to cook and serve them separately. ❜

Put the salt cod to soak for 24 hours, as in the previous recipe. Remove the biggest bones and any thin dark-coloured pieces from the soaked cod, and cut up into thick smaller portions. You may leave the skin on if you wish: some people like it. Put the cleaned pieces into a large saucepan of cold water, bring to the boil, turn the heat down and simmer gently for 30 minutes.

In the meantime, preheat the oven to 190°C/375°F/Gas 5, and make a tomato sauce.

Heat the olive oil in a large pan, and when hot fry the garlic just for a few seconds, then add the tomatoes, salt and pepper. Bring the sauce to simmering, stirring all the time to break up the tomatoes, and cook for 10 minutes. Add the basil leaves at the end.

Drain the salt cod, and arrange the pieces in an ovenproof dish. Cover them with the tomato sauce, season and stew slowly in the preheated oven for an hour, or until the fish is soft. Cover the dish with a lid for the first half-hour. Make sure the fish is always immersed in the sauce, and add a little extra tomato juice or stock as necessary. Serve with boiled potatoes.

Pollo al Forno con Patate
roast chicken with potatoes

 This homely dish is known all over Italy. Chicken used to be a Sunday dish, but is now eaten on any day of the week. As this is an easy recipe, which does not require much preparation time, it is highly suitable for a weekday meal. 9

serves 6

1 roasting chicken weighing 1.3kg (3 lb)

1kg (2¼ lb) medium-sized yellow waxy potatoes, peeled and cut into quarters

1 onion, sliced

2 sprigs fresh rosemary

10 tbsp olive oil

20 garlic cloves, unpeeled

salt and pepper to taste

Preheat the oven to 220°C/425°F/Gas 7.

Clean the chicken and cut it up into 12–16 pieces. Put the chicken pieces together with the potatoes into a baking tray, and mix together with the onion and sprigs of rosemary. Season with salt and pepper and pour over the olive oil. Scatter the garlic cloves on the top and place in the preheated oven. After 20 minutes, turn the heat down to 190°C/375°F/Gas 5. During the roasting time, turn the chicken and potatoes over occasionally so that they cook evenly on all sides. The potatoes should be golden and the garlic crisp after about 1 hour. Serve with salad.

Supreme di Pollo al Limone
chicken escalopes with capers and lemon

> ❝ Chicken meat is very delicate and is suitable for almost any diet. This very Italian way of cooking it contrasts the tenderness of the breast with the intense flavour of the capers and the acidity of the lemon. ❞

serves 4

4 skinless chicken breasts, each sliced into 3 escalopes

plain flour for dusting

1 tbsp capers (salted if possible)

60g (2¼ oz) butter

finely grated rind and juice of 1 large lemon

2 tbsp very finely chopped fresh flat-leaf parsley

salt and pepper to taste

Season the flour with salt and pepper and roll the chicken escalopes lightly in it. Soak the capers in a little water for 20 minutes.

Heat the butter in a large pan and when it is hot, not brown, add the chicken escalopes. Fry gently on each side until they are cooked and golden brown, about 10 minutes. Remove the chicken to a heated serving dish, and keep warm.

Now add the drained capers (chopped if they are large) to the same pan, along with the grated lemon rind and lemon juice. Stir well to deglaze the pan, and add 1–2 tbsp warm water if you like your sauce more liquid. Season with salt and pepper, add the parsley, and pour over the chicken. Serve immediately, accompanied by *French Beans with Tomato* (see page 150).

stuffed chicken legs

6 This was one of my first "professional" recipes, which I created for a *Sunday Times* book written by Lady Arabella Boxer. Since then it has become a classic in my Carluccio delicatessens, and is still going strong. The dish can be prepared well in advance and the chicken legs are equally good served cold. 9

serves 4

4 chicken legs
(the drumstick and thigh)

4 thin slices pancetta or
back bacon

3 tbsp olive oil

For this you require a little manual dexterity! Cut with a small sharp knife into the skin and tendons all around the lower part of the leg, just before the knuckle. Go in deep with the knife until you reach the bone. Still using the same sharp knife, make an incision into the skin and flesh lengthways, until you reach the bone. Detach all the meat from the leg, and open out to obtain a sort of tapering rectangle of flesh, flattened out on your work surface, the (reasonably intact) skin side down.

Make the stuffing by mixing together the breadcrumbs, mortadella, nutmeg, parsley and garlic. Beat the eggs, season with salt and pepper and mix in the other ingredients. Place a spoonful of this mixture in the middle of each rectangle of chicken. Fold the rectangle into a sausage-shaped parcel. Put a piece of bacon lengthways along each 'sausage' to close the join and flap over the end to close the parcel. Bind with kitchen string to make an even shape and so that the stuffing cannot escape.

Meanwhile, preheat the oven to 200°C/400°F/Gas 6.

Heat the oil in a heavy casserole and fry the stuffed chicken legs on all sides, browning them gently. Now place the casserole in the oven and bake for 15–20 minutes. Remove the string and leave the parcels to cool slightly before slicing them. Serve with a simple spinach or potato dish.

Stuffing

55g (2 oz) fresh white
breadcrumbs

75g (2½ oz) mortadella, sliced
and cut into strips

¼ nutmeg, freshly grated

1 tbsp chopped fresh flat-leaf
parsley

1 garlic clove, finely chopped

2 eggs

salt and pepper to taste

pigeons with black olives

serves 4

4 pigeons, complete with giblets

2 tbsp olive oil

salt and pepper to taste

Stuffing

1 small onion, finely chopped

2 tbsp olive oil

the pigeon giblets and liver, chopped

115g (4 oz) fresh pork sausagemeat, crumbled

1 tbsp raisins

175g (6 oz) fresh breadcrumbs

1 tbsp chopped fresh flat-leaf parsley

2 egg yolks

> Tuscany can perhaps be considered the homeland of game. In this region recipes abound for all types of birds, and domestic or wild pigeons are often to be found on the menu. Wood pigeons – which are tastier than bred pigeons – can be ordered from any good butcher or game dealer.

I often stuff birds, game birds in particular, as in my view, stuffing is the simplest, easiest way to make a bird more attractive and flavourful.

Clean and gut the pigeons (taking care not to throw away the giblets). Salt them inside and out, then fry them on all sides in the oil in a large pan for about 15 minutes. Keep the frying oil.

To make the stuffing, fry the onion in the oil in another pan, adding the chopped giblets and liver and the sausagemeat. Continue to fry these ingredients for 15 minutes, then take the pan off the heat and let it cool down a bit. Next add the raisins, breadcrumbs, salt, pepper and parsley. Mix in the egg yolks and then proceed to stuff the pigeons.

For the sauce, use the oil you fried the pigeons in to fry the garlic until golden. Add the wine to deglaze the pan, and reduce a little before adding the tomatoes. (You may need to strain the latter if there seems to be too much liquid.) Cook, stirring, for 5 minutes and then add the olives and seasoning.

Place the stuffed pigeons in a casserole, pour the tomato sauce over them, cover and simmer gently on top of the stove for at least an hour, or until the pigeons are tender. Alternatively, you can put the covered dish in the oven preheated to 200°C/400°F/Gas 6 for an hour, taking the lid off for the last 10 minutes only if the sauce is too liquid. Serve with a simple potato dish.

Sauce

3 garlic cloves, chopped

150ml (5 fl oz) red wine

1 x 425g (15 oz) can peeled plum tomatoes, chopped in the can

20 black olives, pitted

Lepre al Barolo
hare in red wine with grapefruit

serves 8

> ❝ Hare meat has to be marinated overnight, like other types of game, to lessen the "wildness" of the taste. Once the marinade was composed of a sweet and sour mixture, and this idea may still be appreciated today. Chocolate used to be included in sauces in the Tuscan cuisine during the Renaissance, a highly interesting addition which made for a very rich sauce. ❞

1 large hare weighing 2kg (4½ lb), skinned, cleaned and cut into 16 pieces

seasoned plain flour for coating

8 tbsp olive oil

salt and pepper to taste

Marinade

juice of 2 pink grapefruit

500ml (18 fl oz) red wine, preferably Barolo

55g (2 oz) raisins

5 cloves

grated peel of 1 orange

10 bay leaves

1 large sprig fresh thyme

1 sprig fresh rosemary

2 garlic cloves

1 tbsp honey

a bunch of celery leaves

1 large carrot, finely chopped

1 tsp strong (English) mustard

25g (1 oz) dried porcini

Sauce

1 small onion, finely chopped

30g (a good 1 oz) butter

55g (2 oz) prosciutto crudo (Parma ham), sliced and cut into strips

40g (1½ oz) plain bitter chocolate, broken into small pieces

Prepare the marinade by mixing everything together except for the dried porcini. Leave the hare to marinate in it for 24 hours.

Take the hare from the marinade and dry with a cloth. Dust with some seasoned flour and fry in the hot oil on all sides. Heat up the marinade. Remove the pieces of browned hare from the pan and deglaze the pan with a ladleful of the hot marinade.

Place the pieces of hare in a cast-iron casserole and pour over them the deglazed juices and enough marinade to cover, along with the aromatics. Bring to the boil, turn down the heat and simmer gently for 2 hours until the hare is tender. After an hour of cooking, add the dried porcini, crumbled in your hand. (When not soaked first, they will add intense flavour.)

Meanwhile, to make the sauce, fry the onion in the butter until it becomes transparent, then add the prosciutto strips. Take the pieces of hare from the casserole. Strain the liquid and add it to the onion and prosciutto, together with the chocolate. Stir well and simmer for a few minutes longer, seasoning to taste with salt and pepper. Pour the sauce over the hare and serve with grilled or fried polenta (see page 53).

Coniglio San Angelo
rabbit saint angelo

serves 4

1 young rabbit weighing 1kg
(2¼ lb) when cleaned

plain flour for dusting

3 tbsp olive oil

1 garlic clove, sliced

3–4 tomatoes, skinned and
chopped, or 1 x 800g (1¾ lb) can
peeled plum tomatoes

1 sprig each of fresh rosemary
and thyme

150ml (5 fl oz) dry white wine

some fresh basil leaves, torn

salt and pepper to taste

6 This recipe is dedicated to a man who lived alone on an island off the San Angelo locality of Ischia, near Naples. He ran a very small and private restaurant, and was renowned for preparing rabbit in an interesting way. He was also renowned as a ladies' man, and the restaurant was frequented by many German and northern Italian girls, ladies and grannies, obviously in order to enjoy this rabbit dish… I don't know if this man is still living, but I have tried to recreate his recipe as near as possible. 9

Cut the rabbit into smallish pieces and try to take out as many bones as possible. Lightly salt and flour the pieces, then fry them in the oil in a deep saucepan so that every side is well browned. Next add the garlic, the roughly chopped tomatoes, rosemary, thyme and wine. Cook over a moderate heat, with the lid on, for an hour, adding the basil after half an hour. Every now and again stir the sauce and add some of the tomato juice or some water if you find it is getting too thick. Season and serve hot, accompanied by some fried courgettes and boiled new potatoes or wet polenta (see page 53).

roast rabbit with potatoes

serves 6

1 young rabbit weighing about 1kg (2¼lb) when cleaned, cut into chunks

8 tbsp olive oil

seasoned plain flour for coating

100ml (3½ fl oz) dry white wine

2 large onions, finely sliced

1.3kg (3 lb) small new potatoes, scrubbed

3 small sprigs fresh rosemary

salt and pepper to taste

❛ Rabbit meat is similar to chicken in that it is tender and white. It will usually need some additional flavours to make it more interesting: onion and rosemary are ideal. ❜

Preheat the oven to 200°C/400°F/Gas 6.

Put the olive oil into a large casserole, and heat. Coat the rabbit pieces in seasoned flour, and shake off the excess. Fry in the oil until brown on all sides. Deglaze the pan with the wine, then add the onions, potatoes and rosemary, along with some salt and pepper. Cover, put into the preheated oven, and cook for 30 minutes. Give everything a good stir around, then put back in the oven, uncovered, for another 15 minutes or until you see the edges of the potato starting to brown.

Camoscio in Salmì

venison steak with wild mushrooms

❝ This is a typical dish of the Aosta valley region, where it is still possible to hunt deer with a licence that is rather hard to come by. In the rest of Europe it is much easier to find venison, as deer are farmed now in many places. In Italy it is traditional to serve venison with freshly made polenta, which transforms it into a truly magnificent dish. ❞

serves 4

4 x 1cm (½ in) thick slices from a venison leg or fillet, weighing a total of 600g (1 lb 5 oz)

seasoned plain flour for dusting

45g (1½ oz) butter

salt and pepper to taste

Sauce

1 small onion, sliced

115g (4 oz) pancetta affumicata

350g (12 oz) wild mushrooms, cleaned and sliced

Mix the marinade ingredients together and marinate the venison for three days before you want to cook the dish. The meat has to be marinated for quite a long time in order to mute the intensely gamey flavour of the flesh and make it more tender.

Take the meat from the marinade, keeping the marinade to add to the sauce later, and dry with a cloth. Lightly dust the slices with seasoned flour and then fry for 5 minutes in the butter until brown on each side. Put aside and keep hot.

In the same butter, fry the sliced onion and the pancetta pieces. Now add the mushrooms and fry all together for a few minutes until golden. Add 300ml (10 fl oz) of the strained marinade, and allow to bubble and reduce briefly. Add the venison pieces, coat with the sauce, and serve with grilled or fried polenta (see page 53).

Marinade

1.2 litres (2 pints) good red wine

1 small onion, chopped

5 bay leaves

1 sprig fresh rosemary

2 garlic cloves, chopped

2 carrots, chopped

2 celery stalks, chopped

1 sprig fresh thyme

10 juniper berries

1 tbsp black peppercorns, split

Filetto Freddo con Salsa Verde
cold fillet of beef with green sauce

serves 4

1 whole fillet of beef, weighing 600g (1 lb 5 oz) in total

30g (a good 1 oz) butter

salt and pepper to taste

Green sauce

6 tbsp chopped fresh flat-leaf parsley

8 small gherkins

25g (1 oz) salted capers, rinsed

8 anchovy fillets

1 tbsp green peppercorns preserved in brine, drained

grated rind of 1 lemon

6 tbsp olive oil

6 This piece of meat cooked rare and eaten cold resembles the English roast beef, and indeed my love for this dish has made me create an "Italian" version with the addition of a special salsa verde or green sauce. The fillet is the tenderest part of the animal, which makes it eminently suitable for this recipe. 9

Tie the fillet with kitchen string in such a way that it keeps its round shape, and salt it. In a steak pan, heat the butter and fry the whole fillet fiercely for a few minutes on each side, so that it appears almost charred on the outside but is still rare towards the centre. Put it aside to cool.

To make the green sauce the simplest way, put all the ingredients in a blender and purée quite briefly until you have a smooth sauce. Alternatively, chop the parsley, gherkins and capers as finely as you can. Cut the anchovy fillets into small pieces and place them in a mortar. Begin by pounding the anchovies to a paste and then add in this order the green peppercorns, gherkins, capers, lemon peel and parsley. The sauce will now be thick and bitty. At this stage start adding the olive oil, dribble by dribble as for making mayonnaise, until you have a smooth sauce.

Remove the string from the cold fillet. Slice it and arrange the slices on a serving dish, spooning the green sauce around them. In summer, serve this dish with a salad made from new potatoes, and a green salad. Some cannellini or borlotti beans cooked with garlic and oil would make a nice accompaniment, as would some fresh focaccia.

beef steak with pizzaiola sauce

serves 4

❝ La pizzaiola is a classic sauce, probably originating from the ingredients used by the pizza-maker – tomatoes, garlic and oregano cooked in olive oil. La pizzaiola can be equally successfully served with fish such as swordfish and tuna. ❞

500g (1 lb 2 oz) beef sirloin steak cut from the bone into 4 slices, each about 2cm (¾ in) thick

seasoned plain flour for dusting

4 tbsp olive oil

salt and pepper to taste

Salt the meat on both sides and then dip into seasoned flour. Heat the olive oil in a heavy pan over a high heat. Fry the steak as you like it on both sides. Remove from the pan and keep warm.

For the sauce, add the garlic to the olive oil in the pan (add more if need be), reduce the heat a little and, almost immediately, before the garlic starts to brown, add the tomatoes, oregano, capers, anchovies and some salt and pepper to taste. Stir and cook for 5 minutes, incorporating the meat juices into the tomato sauce. Return the steaks to the sauce, and let them soak up the flavour of the tomatoes for a minute before serving, with some fried potatoes (see page 177) and good bread.

Sauce

2 garlic cloves, sliced

1 x 425g (15 oz) can peeled plum tomatoes, chopped in the can

2 pinches of dried oregano

1 tbsp salted capers, rinsed

3 anchovy fillets

meat loaf in tomato sauce

6 I distinctly remember how this dish used to satisfy our appetites when my brothers and I were young. It had two advantages: the sauce in which it was cooked provided an excellent dressing for the pasta which was served up as a first course. Then the meat loaf, cut into slices, appeared as a tasty main course.9

serves 8

1kg (2¼ lb) minced beef

175g (6 oz) breadcrumbs made from stale bread

2 tbsp finely chopped fresh flat-leaf parsley

55g (2 oz) Parmesan, freshly grated

4 eggs

olive oil for shallow-frying

salt and pepper to taste

Mix the minced meat together with the breadcrumbs, parsley, Parmesan, salt and pepper, and thoroughly mix. Lightly beat the eggs and add to the meat mixture, which should now stick together. Form the mass into a large oval meat loaf. If you have difficulty shaping it, and it is falling apart, add a few more breadcrumbs to the mixture. (It is a good idea to fry a small meatball first to check the seasonings.)

In a large oval cast-iron casserole, heat the olive oil and fry the meat loaf until it is a crisp golden brown all over and retains the juices of the meat inside. Take great care not to break the loaf as you turn it in the casserole. Set aside.

In a separate pan make a tomato sauce in the usual way. Season with salt and pepper and add the basil.

Now add the sauce to the meat loaf, put the lid on the casserole and return it to the stove. Simmer gently for about an hour (or bake at 200°C/400°F/Gas 6). Gently turn the loaf from time to time. Remove the lid after 30 minutes to allow the sauce to thicken.

When the loaf is cooked you may use the rich tomato sauce to dress some pasta prepared in the meantime. The meat loaf should be allowed to cool for 10 minutes before it is sliced. Serve with fried potatoes (see page 177).

Tomato sauce

1 onion, finely chopped

4 tbsp olive oil

1 garlic clove

2 x 800g (1¾ lb) cans peeled plum tomatoes, drained of some of their liquid

10 fresh basil leaves, torn

boiled mixed meats from piedmont

serves 8

6 This is perhaps the most famous of all Piedmontese dishes as it invariably figures in most good Italian restaurants abroad. It is a classic autumn or winter dish. In Piedmont there are many ingredients available for the bollito, such as calf's head and feet which, when boiled, will become gelatinous. Make sure to include the famous zampone, a stuffed pig's trotter, which you will find in any good Italian delicatessen. In some regions of Piedmont this dish will be served accompanied by mostarda di Cremona, which is crystallised fruits in a mustard syrup. This is now easy to find as well. 9

1 ox tongue weighing about 1.3kg (3 lb), preferably one that has been soaked in brine

1 boiling chicken weighing about 1.8kg (4 lb)

500g (1 lb 2 oz) beef brisket

1 zampone

1 large sprig fresh rosemary

5 bay leaves

8 medium potatoes

4 carrots, cut into chunks

5 celery stalks, cut into chunks

Clean the ox tongue of any excess fat and gristle. Clean and wash the chicken.

Into a very large saucepan (big enough to take the chicken, tongue and beef), put the ox tongue, cover with cold water and bring to the boil. Skim away the froth that comes to the surface every now and again. Boil the tongue for an hour, then add the piece of beef and the boiling chicken, the rosemary, bay leaves and a little salt. Continue to boil the meats together for a further 2 hours. The boiling chicken and beef should be tested to see if they are cooked after 1½ hours, as it is important that your meats are tender but not falling apart. During the final half-hour of boiling, add your potatoes, carrots, celery and onions.

In a separate saucepan boil your zampone. The cooking time is usually specified on the package, and most zampone are

8 small onions

salt and pepper to taste

Salsa verde

10 anchovy fillets

50 capers

40g (1½ oz) fresh breadcrumbs

a large bunch of fresh flat-leaf parsley

1 garlic clove

2 tbsp white wine vinegar

about 400ml (14 fl oz) olive oil

precooked so that 20 minutes is sufficient. (If cooked from raw, the zampone would take 2–3 hours to become tender!)

When the tongue, chicken and beef are cooked, remove them from the saucepan. Allow the tongue to cool a little before peeling off the skin. Allow all the meats to stand for 10 minutes before carving. Arrange slices of all the different meats on a large hot serving platter. You can ladle a little of the stock on to the platter to keep the meats moist. Arrange the potatoes and other vegetables with the meats, and serve with salsa verde, green sauce.

To make this, put all the ingredients except the olive oil into the blender and mix until you get a thick paste. Then slowly add the olive oil, intermittently blending, until you obtain a beautiful thick sauce. The amount of oil used depends upon the size of your bunch of parsley. You may wish to add salt and pepper, but usually the capers and anchovies are seasoning enough.

Brasato al Nebbiolo
braised beef with red wine

serves 6

> ❝ The Nebbiolo, one of the princes of Italian wines, is supposed to give the maximum flavour to meat and other dishes. Piedmontese beef, full of wonderful taste and tenderness, combines perfectly with the wine, producing this extraordinary dish. ❞

1.3kg (3 lb) rump steak, cut thick in one piece

30g (a good 1 oz) each of butter and lard

1 large onion, sliced

2 garlic cloves, roughly chopped

1 carrot, halved

2 celery stalks, chopped

1 small sprig fresh rosemary

2 bay leaves

1 sprig fresh thyme

5 fresh sage leaves

1 cinnamon stick, 4cm (1½ in) long, or a pinch of ground cinnamon

coarsely grated rind of ¼ lemon

600ml (1 pint) Nebbiolo wine

a little *Beef Stock* (see page 40), optional

salt and pepper to taste

In a heavy casserole just bigger than the piece of steak, heat the butter and lard together. When very hot add the steak and brown on all sides to seal in the juices. Remove the meat and put to one side. Fry the onion, garlic, carrot and celery for a few minutes, then add the herbs, cinnamon, lemon rind and wine. Stir well, deglazing the bottom and sides of the casserole.

Replace the steak in the sauce, season with salt and pepper, and cover the casserole. Simmer very gently for 1½ hours. Turn the steak frequently so that it cooks evenly, and make sure that it is always covered by the sauce. Add a ladle of stock if necessary. When the steak is cooked, leave it to cool.

Strain the sauce to remove the herbs, cinnamon, lemon rind and vegetables. (You may wish to reduce the sauce by increasing the heat and boiling for 5 minutes or more before adding the steak.)

Very gently reheat the steak in the sauce just before serving with new potatoes and a mushroom dish.

veal cutlets with wine and sage

6 Because veal is considered a rather tasteless
meat on its own, it is usually accompanied by
either a herb or a sauce which will enhance the
flavour of the dish. The main virtues of veal,
however, are its tenderness and the facility with
which it is cooked. It is for this reason that most
Italian restaurants have always had a variety
of veal escalopes on their menus. The chop
or nodino of veal is a typical Piedmontese or
Lombardian speciality. The best known is "alla
Sassi", so called because it originated in the Villa
Sassi restaurant, situated in the hills of Turin. 9

serves 4

4 large veal chops, including the
tenderloin

seasoned plain flour for dusting

45g (1½ oz) butter

150ml (5 fl oz) dry white wine

10 fresh sage leaves, roughly
chopped

2 tbsp *Chicken Stock* (see page
40), optional

salt and pepper to taste

Salt the veal and dust with seasoned flour. Heat the butter in a
large pan. When hot, put in the chops and fry over a medium
heat until golden on both sides. This takes about 10 minutes.
Now add the wine, and allow to evaporate before adding the
sage leaves. Turn the heat down and cook gently for a further
10 minutes, adding a little stock to keep the chops moist if
necessary. Season and serve with the juices from the pan (see
the photograph on page 97).

Baked Fennel (see page 171) is an excellent vegetable to serve
as an accompaniment.

Cotoletta alla Milanese
veal cutlet in breadcrumbs

serves 4

4 veal chops with their bones, each weighing 200g (7 oz)

1 egg

5 fresh basil leaves, chopped

4 tbsp freshly grated Parmesan

60g (a good 2 oz) dried breadcrumbs

olive oil for shallow-frying

4 lemon slices

salt and pepper to taste

6 The veal cutlet Milanese, apart from its attached bone, is similar to the equally famous Viennese escalope in that both are coated in breadcrumbs before being fried. But there they start to differ again, especially in their garnishes. And in fact I have deviated slightly from the classic Milanese recipe in that I have added some finely chopped basil and some Parmesan to the egg in which the escalope is dipped. This makes it altogether more interesting! 9

Flatten the chops, leaving the bone, and trim away the fat. Beat the egg, and add the finely chopped basil, grated Parmesan and some salt and pepper. Place the egg in a flat plate, and dip each of the chops into this in turn. Roll them immediately thereafter in the breadcrumbs to thoroughly coat.

Heat the oil in a large pan and fry the chops on both sides over a gentle heat. When the breadcrumbs turn a deep golden colour, take the chops out of the pan and serve garnished with a slice of lemon. Good accompaniments are a *Fried Courgette Salad* (see page 35) or a mixed leaf salad.

Ossobuco Milanese
veal marrow-bone milanese style

serves 4

> ❛This typical speciality of Lombardy, and more precisely of Milan, is a filling dish which is usually eaten during the winter. It's very important to find a butcher who will supply you with the marrow-bones or ossibuchi (so called because they come from the tibia of the calf which, when cut, reveals the bone-marrow). Get him to cut the pieces from the middle of the shin where the bone is rounded on both sides and the meat is dense.❜

4 pieces of veal marrow-bone, 4cm (1½ in) thick (see above)

seasoned plain flour for dusting

4 tbsp olive oil

1 small onion, sliced

1 x 800g (1¾ lb) can peeled plum tomatoes, strained of half their juices

juice of 1 large orange, and finely grated rind of ½ orange

150ml (5 fl oz) dry red wine

salt and pepper to taste

Dust the marrow-bones with seasoned flour. Heat the olive oil in a cast-iron casserole and fry the marrow-bones two at a time on both sides, taking care not to damage the marrow in the centre of the bone or allow it to fall out. Remove the marrow-bones from the casserole and put to one side.

In the same oil, fry the onion until transparent then add the tomatoes, breaking them up in the casserole with a wooden spoon while cooking. Keep the heat up high so that the tomatoes reduce. After 5 minutes add the orange juice, the grated rind and the wine. Continue to cook fast and return the marrow-bones to the sauce. Season the sauce with salt and pepper and then reduce the heat, cover the casserole and simmer for 1–1½ hours until the meat has begun to come away from the bone.

To make the gremolata, simply mix the ingredients together.

Sprinkle each portion with gremolata, and serve with a risotto milanese (see page 50), cooked without the sausage.

Gremolata

4 tbsp finely chopped fresh flat-leaf parsley

1 tbsp finely grated lemon zest

1 small garlic clove, crushed

Stinco di Agnello al Forno
braised lamb shank

> 6 Cooked in this way, the lamb shanks become
> extremely succulent, and the tender pieces of
> meat are wonderful served with some wet
> polenta, rice or a buttery potato purée. These
> types of stew, made with cheaper cuts of meat,
> used to be taken to the central bread oven in the
> middle of the village and left to cook slowly
> when the oven had been turned off after baking
> bread. The baker's reward was generally a
> portion of the stew… 9

serves 4

4 lamb shanks weighing
350–400g (12–14 oz) each

seasoned plain flour for dusting

8 tbsp olive oil

350g (12 oz) mixed carrot,
celery and onion, all prepared
and finely chopped

100ml (3½ fl oz) red wine

200g (7 oz) polpa di pomodoro

2 tbsp tomato purée

salt and pepper to taste

Preheat the oven to 190°C/375°F/Gas 5.

Dust the lamb shanks with seasoned flour, shaking off the excess. Heat the oil in a baking dish or casserole, and fry the shanks until brown on all sides. Add the vegetables, and stir-fry a little. Add the wine, tomato pulp and purée, and some salt and pepper. Stir, cover with foil or a lid, and cook in the preheated oven for 1½ hours. After an hour, look at the shanks and add a little water if needed; stir it in, then continue to cook. Eat hot.

Scottadito
barbecued lamb cutlets

serves 4

12 good best end lamb cutlets

100g (3½ oz) Parma ham fat, very finely minced, or lard

20g (¾ oz) fresh rosemary needles, very finely chopped

1 small garlic clove, crushed

salt and pepper to taste

6 This is a typical Roman recipe whose success depends on two things: some good cutlets from a young lamb and, if possible, a charcoal grill. Apart from these two factors, the secret of this dish lies in its simplicity. It should be eaten with the fingers immediately after being cooked – the Italian word "scottadito" means "burnt fingers"! In some places in Italy, goat or kid is used instead of lamb; you can occasionally find this meat in ethnic markets in Britain. 9

Make a smooth paste from the fat, rosemary, garlic, some salt and plenty of freshly ground black pepper. You can do this in the food processor.

Smear this paste on both sides of the cutlets, and then cook them very quickly over hot charcoal or under a domestic grill. They will need about 3 minutes per side, or more if they are thicker. Eat immediately. A simple tomato salad and some good bread will make excellent accompaniments, or serve with *Fried Peppers* (see page 176) as in the photograph.

noisettes of lamb with artichokes

6 Noisettes are the most tender cut of lamb and, in this recipe, they should be accompanied by equally tender artichokes. It is during the spring that you will be able to find these tender artichokes which, prepared in *Pinzimonio* (see page 180), can even be eaten raw. But you can substitute canned artichoke hearts. 9

serves 4

400g (14 oz) lamb fillet

4 small artichokes

a slice of lemon

4 tbsp olive oil

a bunch of spring onions, trimmed and chopped

55g (2 oz) prosciutto crudo (Parma ham), with fat, cut into strips

a ladleful of stock (see page 40)

1 tbsp capers, preferably salted, rinsed

2 tbsp chopped fresh flat-leaf parsley

salt and pepper to taste

Cut the lamb fillet into 2.5cm (1 in) thick noisettes. Wash the artichokes and pull off the tough outside leaves. Trim off the tops and cut into quarters. If the artichokes have hairy chokes, remove these with a sharp knife. Put the hearts aside in a bowl of cold water with the slice of lemon (to prevent discoloration).

Heat the olive oil in a medium saucepan and fry the noisettes, turning them over so that they brown on each side. Remove them from the pan and place them in a hot dish to keep warm. Add to the pan the spring onions and the prosciutto strips, and fry briefly over a high heat. Add the pieces of artichoke and stir-fry all together for 5–6 minutes. Now add the stock and drained capers, turn the heat down and cook gently for a further 10–15 minutes or until the artichokes are cooked.

Return the noisettes to the pan and add the parsley, pepper and salt (if necessary). Mix the meat with the artichokes, and serve straightaway.

Agnello al Forno con Patate

roast lamb with potatoes

serves 6

1.5kg (2¾ lb) boned shoulder of lamb, cut into medium-sized chunks

1kg (2¼ lb) yellow waxy potatoes (peeled weight), cut into thick slices

3 tbsp black Ligurian olives

1 large onion, sliced

1 sprig fresh rosemary

5 tbsp olive oil

salt and pepper to taste

❝ This is a dish which does not require much in the way of side dishes or other vegetables: it is a meal in itself. But a green vegetable such as broccoli wouldn't go amiss. Even the cooking doesn't involve much work, since the oven does it all. And it is also extremely economical because you can use cheaper cuts of lamb. My father always wanted the head of the lamb, cut in half, to be included in the roasting tray (the only one in the family to do so). What he particularly liked to eat was the brains! ❞

Preheat the oven to 200°C/400°F/Gas 6.

Place the pieces of lamb in a baking tray, then add the potatoes, olives, onion and the rosemary broken into three or four pieces. Pour over the olive oil, season with salt and pepper and then mix everything together with your hands so that both the meat and the potatoes are evenly coated.

Place the baking tray in the preheated oven and bake for 1½ hours. Halfway through cooking, thoroughly stir the ingredients so that the meat and potatoes brown evenly. Serve hot, taking care to give everyone equal portions of potatoes and meat.

grilled lamb steak

serves 4

4 slices of lamb cut from the leg where the bone is quite thin, each slice weighing about 175g (6 oz)

Marinade

1 tbsp each of chopped fresh rosemary, marjoram, flat-leaf parsley and chives

6 tbsp olive oil

juice of 2 lemons

salt and pepper to taste

❝ A good lamb steak cooked over a charcoal grill has an exquisite taste. The meat for this dish needs to be prepared the day before to allow it to become more tender and to absorb all the flavours. ❞

Prepare the marinade by mixing together the chopped herbs with the oil, lemon juice, salt and pepper to taste. Spoon the marinade on to each of the steaks and place them stacked one on top of the other in a small dish. Leave the lamb to marinate in a larder or refrigerator overnight.

The next day, cook the steaks, without any further preparation, on a charcoal grill. They will cook very quickly and be deliciously tender. Serve with a tomato, onion and basil salad or with a French bean salad (see page 185).

pork with preserved peppers

serves 4

400g (14 oz) pork meat plus some fat from various cuts, in small chunks

30g (a good 1 oz) lard

3 tbsp olive oil

200g (7 oz) large red peppers, preserved in vinegar, drained weight, sliced, or 2 small fresh red peppers, de-seeded, plus 2 tbsp red wine vinegar added at the end

4 garlic cloves, cut into slivers

1 dried red chilli, crumbled

salt and pepper to taste

6 This recipe is a classic, very characteristic of the time of year when the pig is slaughtered. Between October and January, the pig is at its peak of condition and at its fattest, and it is then that it must make its ultimate sacrifice… This dish is traditionally cooked with the leftover meats and fats from making salame and ham, and to cut its occasional fattiness, it includes peppers preserved in vinegar. The taste is wonderful, and fresh peppers wouldn't be the same at all (unless treated as below). 9

Heat the lard with the olive oil in a large pan. When very hot add the pieces of pork and fry, turning all the time, for about 10 minutes. Add the red peppers and garlic slivers, and continue to cook over a reduced heat for as long as it takes to cook the garlic, a few minutes only. The preserved red pepper merely requires heating up: the fresh will need at least 10 minutes' cooking. Season the meat mixture with the crumbled red chilli, salt and pepper (and add the vinegar if using fresh peppers). Serve piping hot, with some good bread – and some good red wine!

Arrosto di Maiale
roast pork with garlic

serves 6

1 piece of leg of pork weighing about 1.8kg (4 lb)

4 tbsp olive oil

2 carrots, finely diced

15 garlic cloves, finely chopped

300ml (10 fl oz) dry white wine

sea salt and pepper to taste

6 For this recipe it is best to use the hind leg of the pig (otherwise known as the ham) with its delicious skin. The skin is cut here to let the fat escape and to enable the meat to absorb all the flavours of the fat and seasonings. And, on top of that, it's delicious to eat! 9

Preheat the oven to 220°C/425°F/Gas 7.

Score the skin of the pork with a very sharp knife to make a grid pattern of little squares (your butcher can do this for you). Rub the skin with sea salt and grease on all sides with the olive oil. Place the meat in a baking tray and cook in the preheated oven for 25 minutes.

In the meantime, mix the carrots and garlic with the wine, and season with black pepper.

After roasting the pork for 25 minutes, take it out of the oven and pour over it the carrot, garlic and wine mixture. Don't let the garlic or carrot stick to the skin of the pork, as they will burn. Turn the oven down to 190°C/375°F/Gas 5, replace the roasting pan and cook at this temperature for a further 2 hours. Every now and again baste the pork with the juices in the pan, taking care again not to let the vegetables stick to the skin.

Before carving, leave the meat to rest in its juices for 10 minutes. Accompany with cabbage and mashed potato.

spare ribs with chickpeas

serves 4

1kg (2¼ lb) pork spare-rib chops with plenty of meat on them

250g (9 oz) dried chickpeas, or 2 x 425g (15 oz) cans chickpeas

3 tbsp olive oil

5 garlic cloves, chopped

2 celery stalks, chopped

2 carrots, chopped

1 x 800g (1¾ lb) can peeled plum tomatoes, chopped in the can, or polpa di pomodoro

a little stock (see page 40), optional

5–6 fresh basil leaves, torn

salt and pepper to taste

❝ This dish is typical of Puglia where pulses are very much part of the local cuisine. Many traditional peasant dishes such as this, using pulses like dried beans, broad beans or chickpeas, are now common on the menus of restaurants in the north, where they are attempting to reintroduce such simple and satisfying tastes to their customers. ❞

Put dried chickpeas to soak in a lot of water (remember they will increase their volume threefold) for 24 hours. Strain the chickpeas and add to a saucepan of boiling water (don't add any salt). Boil gently for 1½ hours or until the chickpeas are cooked al dente. Simply drain and rinse the canned chickpeas.

Heat the olive oil in a casserole large enough to take both the chops and the chickpeas. Thoroughly brown the chops; this will take at least 5 minutes on each side. Move them around in the pan so that they do not stick. Add the garlic, celery and carrots to the chops. Fry very briefly, just coating the vegetables with oil, and then add the tomatoes and all their juices, and season with salt and pepper. Cook the chops in the tomato sauce for about 20 minutes, then add the drained chickpeas. If there is not enough liquid to cover both chops and chickpeas, add a ladle of stock or tomato juice.

Cover the pan and simmer for 45 minutes or until the chops are cooked. The meat should be coming away from the bones. Add the basil leaves 5 minutes before serving. Serve with some good home made bread.

Zampone con Lenticchie
stuffed pig's trotter with lentils

6 The stuffed pig's trotter or zampone is a speciality of Modena. The skin of the trotter is stuffed with a selection of minced meats, such as ear and cheek, and spices. The stuffed trotters sold by butchers in Italy require more than 2 hours' cooking time, but you can buy specially packaged products which need to be cooked for only 20 minutes in boiling water. These are available in Italian delicatessens. 9

serves 4

1 zampone weighing about 600g (1 lb 5 oz)

Lentils

400g (14 oz) Castelluccio lentils

a sprig of fresh rosemary

4 sun-dried tomatoes, diced

3 tbsp olive oil

2 garlic cloves, sliced

1 x 425g (15 oz) can peeled plum tomatoes, or polpa di pomodoro

a good pinch of dried oregano

salt and pepper to taste

Put the zampone in a large saucepan of boiling water and simmer for 20 minutes or as instructed on the packaging. In a separate saucepan, simmer the lentils in enough boiling water to cover, along with the rosemary and tomato dice, for 15 minutes. Add a little more water if they have absorbed the first lot.

Meanwhile, in another large pan heat the olive oil and briefly fry the garlic. The moment it begins to turn colour, add the peeled plum tomatoes. Roughly break them up as they fry in the pan. Cook over a medium heat for 10 minutes, reducing the tomatoes to a sauce.

When the lentils are cooked, drain them well and add to the tomato sauce. Season with oregano, salt and pepper. Stir well and continue to cook gently for a further 10 minutes. Test the lentils occasionally: they should not be cooked to a mush, but retain a 'bite'.

Serve the zampone cut into slices 1cm (½ in) thick, with the lentils and possibly some mostarda di Cremona.

calf's liver with butter and sage

serves 4

500g (1 lb 2 oz) calf's liver, cut into 4 slices about 8mm (⅜ in) thick

seasoned plain flour for dusting

45g (1½ oz) butter

12 fresh sage leaves

salt and pepper to taste

❝ I don't know if this can even be classified as a recipe, it is so simple. All I know is that it is found on the menus of most Italian restaurants, for the combination of liver and sage is so delicious. ❞

Season the pieces of liver on both sides and then dust with seasoned flour. Heat the butter in a large pan. Fry the liver slices in the butter, only a couple of minutes on each side. Add the sage when you have cooked one side.

Any kind of delicate vegetable can accompany the liver – some sautéed spinach or *Zucchini alla Scapece* (see page 35) would be ideal. (See the photograph on page 147.)

Fegato alla Veneziana
calf's liver venetian style

serves 4

400g (14 oz) calf's liver, sliced into thin strips

300g (10½ oz) onions, coarsely sliced

6 tbsp olive oil

seasoned plain flour for coating

2 tbsp white wine vinegar

1 tbsp finely chopped fresh flat-leaf parsley

salt and pepper to taste

6 This typical Venetian recipe has become a classic Italian dish, found on Italian restaurant menus all over the world. 9

Fry the onions slowly in a large pan with the olive oil until transparent, but do not let them burn. When cooked, remove the onions from the pan, draining them of oil, and put to one side. Roll the strips of liver in seasoned flour and shake off the excess. Fry in the oil remaining in the onion pan over a medium heat, turning frequently, for 5 minutes. Return the onions to the pan, and season with salt and pepper. Add the wine vinegar, which should be left to reduce a little, no more than a minute.

Serve with a sprinkling of parsley and something like a fennel salad.

Trippa alla Genovese
tripe genoese style

6 All the different kinds of offal represent true delicacies for countries such as France and Italy. In Britain and the USA, however, fanatics for things like tripe, sweetbreads and brains are decidedly less numerous, which is a pity. Tripe (or "busecca", as it is called in Milan) is part of the cow's stomach, and it can be truly delicious if cooked properly. Before being sold it is blanched to a creamy white by being boiled for a short period. 9

serves 4

500g (1 lb 2 oz) fine-textured tripe (honeycomb)

2 celery stalks

4 shallots

2 garlic cloves

1 carrot

45g (1½ oz) lard

3 tbsp olive oil

150ml (5 fl oz) dry white wine

1 litre (1¾ pints) *Chicken Stock* (see page 40)

1 tbsp chopped fresh flat-leaf parsley

5–6 fresh basil leaves, torn

55g (2 oz) Parmesan, freshly grated

salt and pepper to taste

Clean the tripe and dry it with a cloth. Chop the celery, shallots and garlic, and cut the carrot into strips.

Heat the lard and oil in a heavy casserole with a lid, and gently fry the shallots, celery and carrot together for a few minutes. Add the garlic, and before it turns colour, add the wine. Allow the wine to bubble for a minute, and then add the tripe and the stock, cover the casserole, and simmer gently for at least 1½ hours (the tripe should be slightly al dente). Just before serving, add the parsley, basil, salt and pepper. Serve in soup bowls with a generous sprinkling of grated Parmesan.

Rognoni di Vitello Trifolati

calf's kidneys with garlic and parsley

6 The word "trifolati" originally indicated the addition of truffles (from the Piedmontese "trifola", meaning truffle). As the truffle is a rare – and expensive – commodity the word has assumed a secondary, more popular meaning – denoting that something is fried together with butter, garlic and parsley. However, if you do happen to come across some truffles, you could add a couple of slices to this dish, which would enhance the flavours immeasurably. 9

serves 4

600g (1 lb 5 oz) calf's kidneys

seasoned plain flour for coating

45g (1½ oz) butter

2 garlic cloves, sliced

75ml (2½ fl oz) dry white wine

2 tbsp chopped fresh flat-leaf parsley

salt and pepper to taste

Thoroughly clean the kidneys, removing all the fat and gristle from the middle. Slice them finely, then roll them in the seasoned flour. Brush off any excess, then fry the kidney slices in the hot butter over a high heat for about 5 minutes, turning constantly. Add the garlic and lightly fry for a moment or so. Next add the wine and some salt and pepper and allow to reduce for a minute or so. Just before serving, sprinkle with the parsley.

Accompany with a vegetable such as spinach or fried potatoes and a green salad (see pages 168 and 177).

Animelle con Limone e Capperi
sweetbreads with lemon and capers

serves 4

> 6 This combination successfully contrasts the richness of the sweetbreads with the flavours of the lemon and capers. This remains one of the favourite recipes in my Neal Street restaurant. Not many butchers will automatically stock calf's sweetbreads, but you should be able to order them, if you give the butcher good notice (and he is a good butcher!). 9

400g (14 oz) calf's sweetbreads

seasoned plain flour for dusting

55g (2 oz) butter

25g (1 oz) salted capers, soaked in water

juice of 1 lemon

1 tbsp chopped fresh flat-leaf parsley

salt and pepper to taste

Prepare the sweetbreads by soaking them in cold water for about an hour, so that most of the blood is removed. Bring a small saucepan of water to the boil and poach the sweetbreads for a couple of minutes. Remove from the boiling water and leave to cool before removing the skin and nerves. Cut into slices.

Dust the slices of sweetbread in the seasoned flour. Heat the butter in a pan until it fizzes. Add the sweetbreads and fry over a gentle heat until a good golden colour on each side. Drain the capers well and add them to the sweetbreads along with the lemon juice. Serve immediately with the sauce from the pan, sprinkled with chopped parsley.

Opposite foreground: *Animelle con Limone e Capperi.* Background: *Fegato Burro e Salvia* (see page 142).

Vegetali e Insalate
vegetables and salads

Italians use lots of vegetables in their cooking, and do so according to the seasons because most vegetables and salad ingredients are produced locally. Artichokes are the first to arrive, and they last until mid May. They can be stuffed, roasted, deep-fried or eaten raw, and can also be used in risotto and soup. Asparagus is next in season, and it can be boiled and topped with ham, with melted butter and Parmesan, with scrambled eggs or with vinaigrette, or used in tarts, risottos and pasta sauces. Fagiolini (green beans) and fagioli (pulses like borlotti beans) are the next to come, followed closely by peppers and tomatoes, courgettes and aubergines. Wild mushrooms and truffles mark the start of the autumn season.

A winter vegetable that has become increasingly familiar over the last few years is the radicchio di treviso, a versatile leaf of the chicory family. Long in shape like cos lettuce, it is cultivated in Treviso in the Veneto, and it is closely related to the little round, red radicchio used more normally in salads. And then there are the cabbages, including Savoy and the new cavolo nero, or black cabbage, and pumpkins and the many wonderful root vegetables.

Italian salads are artful mixtures of cultivated and wild plants: one salad may contain ten, or even more, different types of foliage. The dressing will be simple – a good olive oil with lemon juice or either wine vinegar or balsamic vinegar, and sometimes garlic or onion will be added or a handful of fresh herbs.

The salad is never eaten by itself. It is usually served as part of il secondo, although some people eat the cheese and salad together. And it is very rarely served as an antipasto: the most notable exceptions are *Pinzimonio* and *Bagna Cauda* (see pages 180 and 187).

Opposite: *Finocchi Gratinati* (see page 171).

Fagiolini alla Napoletana
french beans with tomato

serves 4

500g (1 lb 2 oz) very tender French beans, topped and tailed

4 tbsp olive oil

2 garlic cloves, finely chopped

600g (1 lb 5 oz) ripe tomatoes, skinned and chopped,
or 1 x 800g (1¾ lb) can peeled plum tomatoes, chopped in the can

10 fresh basil leaves, torn

salt and pepper to taste

Crostini

4 slices good country bread, toasted

❝ This excellent marriage of typically Neapolitan ingredients provides a simple but delicious starter, which can also be eaten, without the crostini, as an accompaniment to a main course, either hot or cold (see the photograph on page 113). ❞

Heat the olive oil in a saucepan, and add the chopped garlic. Don't let it colour: just fry for 30 seconds or less. Add the tomatoes to the oil and garlic. Cook fiercely for 5 minutes, reducing the liquid, then add the beans and some salt. Cover the pan, reduce the heat and simmer for 5–10 minutes or until the beans are al dente. Shortly before the end of cooking, add the basil leaves and some black pepper. Serve as a starter on the crostini.

fried sweet baby peppers

serves 4

6 A recipe typical of southern Italy, using small peppers which are similar in look to chilli peppers. They are green, about 7.5cm (3 in) long, and very sweet in flavour. The whole pepper is eaten, even the seeds, as they are very tender. If you buy the peppers outside Italy, do make sure they are the right ones – cooking chillies in this recipe would be disastrous! Sometimes they can be found in markets abroad, but in Italy they are commonplace and are called "peperoncini". They should be served as a side dish with good bread such as fresella (see page 182). 9

600g (1 lb 5 oz) sweet baby peppers (peperoncini)

6 tbsp olive oil

2 garlic cloves, chopped

salt and pepper to taste

Heat the olive oil in a heavy pan and when hot put in the peppers. Fry for 5 minutes, stirring from time to time, so that the peppers fry on each side. Their skins will begin to blister, and at this point add the garlic. Fry gently for a few minutes until the garlic begins to turn golden. Add some salt and pepper, and serve hot or cold.

Pomodori Ripieni di Riso
tomatoes stuffed with rice

serves 4

4 ripe beef tomatoes (preferably taller than fatter)

55g (2 oz) long-grain rice

1 tbsp each of chopped fresh chives, mint and basil

3 tbsp olive oil

salt and pepper to taste

❛ A typically Roman recipe cooked in various ways with different ingredients, but always with excellent results. I also like to eat this dish cold as a starter. ❜

Preheat the oven to 200°C/400°F/Gas 6.

Cut the tops off the tomatoes to form lids. Without breaking the tomatoes, scoop out the insides with a teaspoon. Chop the insides, keeping the seeds. Mix the rice with the chopped herbs, salt, pepper and the chopped insides of the tomatoes. Add to this mixture 2 tbsp of the olive oil, and use to stuff the tomato shells. Put on the lids, and place in an ovenproof dish. Sprinkle the remaining oil over the top, and bake in the preheated oven for about 45 minutes, basting occasionally with the juices in the pan.

Melanzane e Peperoni Ripieni
stuffed peppers and aubergines

6 My mother was always good at making this recipe. I remember it was delicious in summer when the heat was intense and it wasn't so necessary to eat large quantities of protein. This dish was nearly always served cold, but still crispy on the top, and accompanied by bread, even though the filling contained breadcrumbs. She used to prepare more than was needed. This was greatly appreciated by my brother and me at around one in the morning, when we returned from our summer escapades to raid the fridge! 9

serves 4

2 large yellow or red sweet peppers

2 medium aubergines

olive oil

400g (14 oz) ripe tomatoes, skinned and finely chopped

45g (1½ oz) capers (salted if possible), rinsed and finely chopped

12 anchovy fillets, finely chopped

2 garlic cloves, very finely chopped

4 tbsp finely chopped fresh flat-leaf parsley

85g (3 oz) fresh white breadcrumbs

55g (2 oz) Parmesan, freshly grated

3 grates of nutmeg

Preheat the oven to 200°C/400°F/Gas 6.

Slice each of the peppers and the aubergines in two lengthways. Remove the stalks and the seeds from the peppers, leaving a clean cavity for the filling. Scoop out as much as you can of the flesh of the aubergine with a knife, taking care to leave the skin intact. Get rid of as many seeds as you can. Chop the scooped-out pulp finely and fry it in 2 tbsp oil for 5–6 minutes, until soft. Remove from the heat and leave to cool.

Mix the tomatoes, capers, anchovies, garlic and parsley with the breadcrumbs, Parmesan, nutmeg and the aubergine pulp, including the oil in which it was cooked. Fill the aubergine and pepper shells with this mixture.

Put 1 tbsp oil in the bottom of an oven dish large enough to hold the eight halves and arrange them in it. Pour 4 more tbsp oil over the stuffed vegetables and bake in the hot oven for about 40 minutes. Serve hot or cold.

La Parmigiana di Melanzane
baked aubergine with cheese and tomato

serves 8 as a main course,

10–12 as a starter

4 large aubergines weighing altogether 1.1–1.2kg (about 2½ lb)

plain flour for coating

4 eggs

plenty of olive oil

300g (10½ oz) fontina cheese, sliced

115g (4 oz) Parmesan, freshly grated

salt and pepper to taste

❝ I've never known whether this dish is called "parmigiana" because it comes from Parma, or because it's made with Parmesan cheese. It is originally from Sicily, but it is cooked all over Italy and can be an excellent vegetarian main course. I've changed the classic recipe slightly. You could use courgettes instead of the aubergines. ❞

Slice the aubergines about 1cm (½ in) thick. Dust the slices on both sides with flour. Beat the eggs, season with salt, and dip the floured aubergine slices into this. Fry the aubergine slices three or four at a time in some hot oil. Brown on both sides, remove and drain on kitchen paper. You will need more oil from time to time.

Now make your tomato sauce in the usual way, adding salt, pepper and the basil towards the end.

Preheat the oven to 200°C/400°F/Gas 6.

Put two or three spoonfuls of tomato sauce in the bottom of a large ovenproof dish, then arrange a layer of the aubergine slices, placed as close together as possible. Cover the aubergines with some pieces of fontina, spoon a little tomato sauce on the cheese and sprinkle with some of the Parmesan. Continue with another layer of aubergine slices, arranging them in the opposite direction to the layer below, cover with fontina, tomato sauce and Parmesan. The final layer should be of tomato sauce, small pieces of fontina and a generous amount of Parmesan. Bake in the preheated oven for 25–30 minutes. Leave the dish to sit for 15 minutes before cutting up to serve.

Sauce

4 tbsp olive oil

1 garlic clove, chopped

1½ x 800g (1¾ lb) cans peeled plum tomatoes, chopped in the can

10 fresh basil leaves, torn

Asparagi alla Milanese
asparagus with fried eggs

serves 4

600g (1 lb 5 oz) fresh asparagus, peeled

40g (1½ oz) butter

8 large eggs

30g (a good 1 oz) Parmesan, freshly grated

salt and pepper to taste

❛ If Italians ate savoury dishes for breakfast as the British do, then this would be perfect. Having lived abroad for two-thirds of my life, wandering through Europe, I have learned to eat a "proper" breakfast, and this is what I choose in spring. ❜

Boil the asparagus in slightly salted water for 15–20 minutes, or until tender, according to size. Drain well.

Meanwhile, melt the butter in a large pan, and then fry the eggs until the whites have set well.

Place the asparagus on hot plates, and top with 2 eggs per portion. Season to taste, and sprinkle with the Parmesan. Serve immediately.

Carciofi in Umido
stewed artichokes

serves 4

1kg (2¼ lb) fresh artichokes

juice of ½ lemon

8 tbsp olive oil

55g (2 oz) pancetta affumicata or smoked bacon, cut into matchsticks

400g (14 oz) onions, finely sliced

2 garlic cloves, sliced

45g (1½ oz) capers, preferably salted, rinsed

2 tbsp chopped fresh flat-leaf parsley

salt and pepper to taste

6 Small tender artichokes can now be found outside Italy, although I still think those in Italy are best. Importers are gradually coming to realise that we can do more in this country than boil large artichokes and serve them with melted butter or hollandaise. Which is just as well, as there are so many recipes in the Italian canon which use small artichokes. 9

Clean the artichokes, pulling off all the tough outer leaves. Cut off the tops and the stalks about 2.5cm (1 in) from the base. (If the artichokes are large, cut them in half and then in quarters, cutting away the hairy choke with a sharp knife.) Put the prepared artichokes in a bowl of water with the lemon juice, to prevent discoloration.

In a medium saucepan heat the olive oil, add the bacon matchsticks and fry for a couple of minutes. Then add the onions, and when they begin to colour add the garlic and capers. Cook together just for a minute over a medium heat before adding the artichokes and a ladle of hot water. Season with salt and pepper and turn the heat down low. Cover and simmer for 20 minutes or until the artichokes are cooked. Bigger ones take longer – up to 40 minutes. Add the chopped parsley before serving. This dish is also excellent cold.

Torta di Patate
potato cake

serves 6

2kg (4½ lb) good floury potatoes

85g (3 oz) butter

55g (2 oz) Parmesan, freshly grated

4 grates of nutmeg

4 eggs, beaten well

115g (4 oz) fontina cheese or any other soft cheese

115g (4 oz) cooked ham or salami, or both mixed

20g (¾ oz) dried breadcrumbs

salt and pepper to taste

6 This was originally a "poor man's cake" in the south of Italy, which was made for picnics, or simply as a vehicle to use up leftovers. Now, however, the ingredients are often bought specially, as it is so delicious. 9

Peel and boil the potatoes. When cooked, mash them thoroughly and mix with half the butter, the grated Parmesan, nutmeg, eggs, and some salt and pepper.

Preheat the oven to 200°C/400°F/Gas 6.

Butter a deep ovenproof dish, and place in it half the potato mixture. Cut the fontina into thin slices and the ham and salami into strips. Cover the potato with the cheese, salami and ham, and dot with some of the remaining butter. Put the remainder of the potato mixture on top, dot with the rest of the butter, shake the breadcrumbs over, and bake for 25 minutes in the preheated oven. Serve after cooling for 5–10 minutes.

Carciofi alla Giudea
artichokes the jewish way

serves 4

12 tender medium artichokes

12 garlic cloves

as much good olive oil as is needed to cover the artichokes, about 400ml (14 fl oz)

1 tsp salt

3 tbsp chopped fresh flat-leaf parsley

❝ A typically Roman recipe, which is Jewish in origin. It is very easy to prepare, but bear in mind it requires a lot of good olive oil which will add flavour to the artichokes. Any leftover oil can be used for other purposes – though it will be slightly flavoured by the artichokes, and coloured slightly more green. ❞

Clean the artichokes: pull off the tough outside leaves, cut off the tips, and peel away with a knife any dark green left at the base of the bud. Cut the stalks about 5cm (2 in) from the head. Now halve the artichokes and if they are large, cut into quarters. With a sharp knife cut away any hairy choke at the centre. If you find very small artichokes, the size of an apricot, then cook them whole.

Peel the garlic. If you squeeze it gently between the palms of your hands, the skin comes off easily.

Put the garlic and artichokes in a pan with a tight-fitting lid and cover with the olive oil. (If you pack the artichokes tightly, you will save on oil!) Add the salt, put on the lid and very gently heat up the oil. Cook on a low heat for 40 minutes: the oil must not be allowed to fry, and the garlic must not brown. Drain off the oil, add the parsley and serve immediately – but the artichokes are also good cold as an antipasto.

Torta Pasqualina
easter cake

serves 8

650g (1 lb 7 oz) ready-made puff pastry, defrosted if frozen

milk for glazing

Filling

3 tbsp olive oil

55g (2 oz) pancetta affumicata or smoked bacon, cut into matchsticks

1 garlic clove, finely chopped

2 ripe tomatoes, skinned and roughly chopped

750g (1 lb 10 oz) bitter leaves (curly endive, radicchio, batavia etc.), cut into 6cm (2½ in) lengths

25g (1 oz) capers, preferably salted, rinsed

500g (1 lb 2 oz) ricotta cheese

10 eggs

55g (2 oz) Parmesan, freshly grated

salt and pepper to taste

❛ This Genoese speciality is ideal for picnics; in fact the Italians cook it for the traditional trip to the country on the day after Easter, which is called Paquetta. ❜

Heat the olive oil in a large saucepan that has a tight-fitting lid. Fry the bacon in the hot oil and after a minute add the garlic. The bacon must become quite crisp and the garlic must not go brown. Add the tomatoes and when they have begun to bubble put in the bitter leaves and capers. Stir so that all the ingredients are well mixed. Cover the pan and simmer for 15 minutes. The leaves should be cooked. Drain away any excess liquid and put aside to cool.

Preheat the oven to 190°C/375°F/Gas 5.

In the meantime, roll out the pastry into two large rectangles, one large enough to fit inside a baking tray about 20 x 30cm (8 x 12 in) and at least 7cm (2¾ in) deep; the other slightly smaller for the top. Line the baking tray with the larger piece of pastry and trim the top and sides.

Now beat the ricotta cheese with a fork, add two of the eggs and continue to beat until the mixture becomes lighter. Add the Parmesan, salt, pepper and finally the cooked leaf mixture. Gently mix together and then spoon into the pastry case.

Make eight wells in the ricotta mixture and break an egg into each. Season the top with salt and pepper before covering with the second piece of pastry, pricking holes here and there to allow steam to escape. Be careful not to prick holes in the pastry where the eggs are or you will break the yolks. Decorate the top with strips of pastry, brush with milk, and bake in the preheated oven for 45–60 minutes. The pie can be served hot or cold.

Cocozielli e Ova

courgette and egg

serves 4

400g (14 oz) courgettes, cut in thin slices

1 large onion, sliced

5 tbsp olive oil

55g (2 oz) Parmesan, freshly grated

8 eggs, beaten

salt and pepper to taste

❝ The title is Neapolitan dialect, and it implies something simple, able to be cooked by anybody, but also something delicious, that costs nothing to make (or very little). The dish is refreshing in summer, served with bread and a few salad leaves. ❞

Fry the onion in the oil first for 5 minutes, then add the courgettes and continue frying to soften and lightly colour.

Add the Parmesan to the eggs, and season with salt and pepper. When the courgettes and onion are ready, pour in the eggs, and stir to scramble. Serve hot.

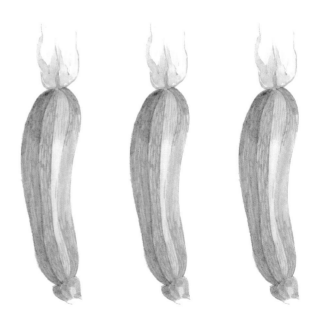

Fritto Misto di Vegetali
fried mixed vegetables

serves 6

1kg (2¼ lb) prepared mixed vegetables

corn oil or olive oil, or a mixture of both, for deep-frying

3 lemons, cut into wedges

Batter

125g (4½ oz) plain flour

4 large eggs

75ml (2½ fl oz) beer or lager

salt to taste

6 This is the Italian version of tempura. Vegetables that can be used raw include courgette flowers; spinach and Swiss chard; quartered radicchio; sliced aubergines; mushrooms and small artichokes which have been cleaned and trimmed. Cut courgettes lengthways into slices. 9

Firmer-textured vegetables need blanching beforehand to make them tender before frying. Asparagus stalks can be kept whole; celeriac, celery, fennel and Jerusalem artichokes should be sliced. Separate cauliflower and broccoli into florets.

With the exception of mushrooms, which simply need wiping, all the vegetables should be washed and thoroughly drained dry before being dipped in the batter.

Take a combination of four or five different vegetables and prepare them as described above. Heat the oil in a deep-fryer. To save oil, don't use a very large pan, which would require at least 5cm (2 in) oil.

Make the batter by sieving the flour into a large bowl, add the eggs to the centre and mix gently, incorporating the flour. When all the flour is blended with the egg, making sure it is free of lumps, add the beer and some salt. Mix thoroughly.

Dip the vegetables in the batter, allow any excess to drip off, then deep-fry in the hot oil until golden. Drain on kitchen paper and serve with lemon wedges.

grilled cep caps

6 I think everyone may be aware by now that I am fanatical about collecting wild mushrooms! In the 26 years I have lived in London, there have been many changes in the supply of wild mushrooms. Now it is not only fashionable to have a selection of them on the menu of many restaurants, you can also buy them in specialist food shops. You don't really have to go into the woods any more to pick your own (although for me, that's half the fun!). However, if you do want to try your hand at mushroom hunting, then I suggest that you join a mycological society, which will provide you with all the necessary knowledge. 9

serves 4

4 x 10cm (4 in) cep caps, or
8 x 5cm (2 in) cep caps, or
4 large open field mushrooms

2 tbsp olive oil

salt and pepper to taste

The wonderful flavour from grilling over charcoal comes from the oil dripping down on to the hot coals and the resulting fragrant smoke penetrating the mushrooms. If you can't get hold of any ceps, use large open field mushroom caps.

Clean the ceps by wiping or brushing them rather than washing them. Cut off the stems and use them for another recipe. Preheat the grill.

Brush the top surface of the caps with oil and sprinkle with salt. Place top side upwards on the grill and grill for about 4–5 minutes. Turn the caps over, pour the remainder of the olive oil into the centre of each, sprinkle again with salt and continue to grill until cooked. According to their size they may take up to 10 minutes. Season with black pepper.

curly endive and cannellini beans

serves 4–6

200g (7 oz) dried cannellini beans, or 1 x 425g (15 oz) can cannellini beans

400g (14 oz) curly endive, batavia or dandelion leaves, washed

6 tbsp olive oil

4 garlic cloves, sliced

2 small dried red chillies, crumbled

600ml (1 pint) water

salt and pepper to taste

6 This is a good accompaniment for stronger tasting meats such as pork or lamb. I use wild field chicory which is related to dandelion, but you can use any bitter leaves such as batavia, curly endive or frisée. 9

Put the dried beans to soak for 12 hours or more in a large bowl (they increase in size). Drain them and boil for 2 hours in fresh unsalted water. Salt at the end of the cooking time. If using canned beans drain them from their liquid and rinse them before use. Wash the endive and cut it up into short lengths.

Heat the olive oil in a large saucepan, fry the garlic without browning, and then add the endive and chillies. Keeping the heat high, stir-fry for a minute or two, coating the endive with the oil, then add the drained cannellini beans, some salt and the water. If you are using canned beans, you will find that they absorb less liquid, so reduce the amount of water slightly. Bring to the boil, cover the saucepan and reduce the heat. Simmer until the endive is tender and most of the liquid has evaporated, but the consistency is still slightly soupy.

Piselli con Cipolle e Prosciutto

peas with onion and ham

serves 4

300g (10½ oz) fresh podded peas, or frozen

3 tbsp olive oil

1 small white onion, finely sliced

150g (5½ oz) cooked ham, diced

salt and pepper to taste

❝ This recipe enhances the ordinary frozen garden pea by cooking it in olive oil with onion and adding pink cooked ham. A very characteristic and complementary Italian combination, the dish can accompany both meat and fish. ❞

Heat the olive oil in a medium saucepan and fry the onion for a few minutes. When it begins to colour, add the fresh peas, stir and cook for 5 minutes on a low heat (8–10 if frozen). Add the ham, salt and pepper, and stir over the heat for a minute or so, mixing well together.

Bietole al Burro
swiss chard with butter

> Whenever possible, I try to avoid cooking vegetables in water and then putting butter on them. Instead, I prepare them in a way that conserves the vitamin content which remains in the cooking liquid and enhances their flavour at the same time. Swiss chard is a very characteristic Italian vegetable, which is like two vegetables in one – its stalks, which are crisp, and its leaves, which taste a little like spinach.

serves 4

500g (1 lb 2 oz) Swiss chard, with stalks

45g (1½ oz) butter

100ml (3½ fl oz) water or stock

salt and pepper to taste

Wash and cut the chard, including the stalks, into 2.5cm (1 in) slices. Heat the butter in a large saucepan, and when melted add the chard. Increase the heat and stir to combine the butter with the chard, then add the water or stock and some salt. Cover the pan and cook for about 7 minutes, or until tender. If there is too much liquid, take the lid off and continue to cook to let the water evaporate a little. Sprinkle with pepper before serving.

Spinaci, Olio e Limone

spinach with oil and lemon

serves 4

600g (1 lb 5 oz) spinach

3 tbsp extra virgin olive oil

juice of ½ lemon

salt and pepper to taste

6 This is one of the best ways of using an oil and lemon dressing. The oil gives a certain softness, and the sharpness of the lemon brings out the flavour of the vegetable. 9

Wash the spinach thoroughly and leave whole, removing only the toughest stalks. In a large saucepan bring 5cm (2 in) of salted water to the boil, then add the spinach and cook for 2 minutes (less if the leaves are small and tender). Drain immediately and pour over it the oil mixed with the lemon juice. Add lots of freshly ground black pepper, and serve.

Carote Fritte
fried carrots

serves 4

600g (1 lb 5 oz) carrots, peeled weight

3 tbsp olive oil

4 garlic cloves, unpeeled

2 tbsp finely chopped fresh flat-leaf parsley

salt to taste

6 Frying unpeeled garlic cloves along with the carrots imparts a wonderful flavour to them, much less pungent than you might imagine. This dish goes very well with the spinach dish opposite. 9

Wash and slice the carrots lengthways. Bring a saucepan of salted water to the boil, add the carrots, and cook, just boiling, for 7–8 minutes. Drain well.

Heat the olive oil in a frying pan and gently fry the carrots with the unpeeled garlic until brown, about 10–12 minutes. Both carrots and garlic should be tender. Add the parsley and serve.

turnip shoots with garlic and oil

6 This inexpensive dish has a slightly bitter taste that doesn't appeal to everyone. But, served with a good steak, especially a charcoal-grilled one, it is extraordinary. Try to buy tender turnip (or rape) shoots; only the tops are used, as the main part is tough. If you cannot find this vegetable, then various others could be prepared in the same way: broccoli or sprouting broccoli, cauliflower, spinach, Swiss chard or even French beans. You can also boil the vegetables until tender, drain them and pour over them the oil flavoured with the fried garlic and chilli. 9

serves 4

900g (2 lb) turnip or rape tops, cleaned

6 tbsp olive oil

4 garlic cloves, sliced

2 small dried red chillies, crumbled

salt to taste

Wash the turnip tops very thoroughly and cut away any tough stalks or leaves. Steam or boil in salted water for only 3–4 minutes, then drain.

Heat the olive oil in a large pan, and fry the garlic until it begins to colour. Add the chillies and turnip tops. Stir-fry for a few minutes, season with salt, and serve immediately.

Finocchi Gratinati
baked fennel

serves 6

1kg (2¼ lb) fennel bulbs

45g (1½ oz) butter

4 grates of nutmeg

2 tbsp dry breadcrumbs

salt and pepper to taste

❝ Fennel is extraordinarily versatile. Not only can it be cooked as in this delicious dish to accompany both meat and fish, it can also be eaten raw after a meal as a digestif or raw in salads. Along with other vegetables, it can also be dipped into a bowl of extra virgin olive oil in *Pinzimonio*, or into *Bagna Cauda* (see pages 180 and 187). Choose round, fat, firm fennel bulbs. ❞

Wash and clean the fennel bulbs. Cut off the top stalks and the hard base, and cut each bulb in four lengthways. Boil the fennel quarters in salted water for 15 minutes, drain and leave to cool a bit. Meanwhile, preheat the oven to 200°C/400°F/Gas 6.

Butter an ovenproof dish, and place the fennel pieces in it, side by side. Dot with pieces of butter, season with salt, pepper and nutmeg, and sprinkle with the breadcrumbs. Bake in the preheated oven for 15–20 minutes until golden and crisp on top. (See also the photograph on page 149.)

Cicoria Vestita
dressed chicory

> In Italy we use quite a few vegetables belonging to the chicory family. The large green frizzy leaves we stew, while dandelion leaves are eaten raw in salads. The radicchio more commonly known here now as trevise, we even grill. We are very fond of the slightly bitter taste of these vegetables. The chicory used here is the Belgian variety, the long buds of which are blanched during growing so they remain pale in colour. This combination with ham can be eaten hot or cold, used as an antipasto, as a side dish for meat or fish, or as a main course, depending on your appetite.

serves 4

4 heads Belgian chicory

8 slices prosciutto cotto (cooked ham), not too thick

4 tbsp olive oil

salt and pepper to taste

Preheat the oven to 190°C/375°F/Gas 5.

Cut each head of chicory in half and blanch in boiling salted water for 5 minutes. Drain well and wrap each half in a slice of ham. Line the halves up against each other snugly in a casserole. Sprinkle with salt and pepper and the olive oil, then cover with the lid or foil, and braise in the preheated oven for 20 minutes.

Peperonata
stewed peppers

serves 4

1 medium onion

2 large red sweet peppers

2 celery stalks, with leaves

4 ripe tomatoes

5 tbsp olive oil

salt and pepper to taste

This is a typically Piedmontese dish based on peppers, tomatoes, onions and celery. You could add garlic to the mix if you liked, and a final garnish of fresh basil leaves. Peperonata is usually eaten as a side dish with meat or fish but, perhaps curiously, it is also served as an accompaniment to polenta.

Prepare the vegetables. Chop the onion, seed and dice the red peppers, slice the celery, and skin and roughly chop the tomatoes.

Heat the oil in a large frying pan. When hot, fry the onion until it begins to turn colour then add the peppers and celery. Fry together for 2–3 minutes. Now add the tomatoes and turn the heat down so that you slowly simmer the vegetables until they are reduced and resemble a ratatouille. This may take 35–40 minutes. Season with salt and pepper and serve either hot or cold.

red and yellow peppers preserved in vinegar

❝ My mother used to have a "damigiana" or demijohn with a huge cork about 15cm (6 in) across. In the late summer she used to fill the whole jar with special fleshy, round red peppers like huge tomatoes. She preserved them whole, not cut into pieces as I suggest below. The amount my mother made lasted our family the whole winter. We usually ate them dressed with beautiful virgin olive oil and also as an accompaniment to pork dishes. ❞

fills a 1.2 litre (2 pint) preserving jar

3–4 red and yellow sweet peppers weighing in total 800g (1¾ lb)

1.7 litres (3 pints) white wine vinegar

1 spray fresh bay leaves

salt to taste

Greenhouse cultivated peppers can of course be used in this recipe, but the Italian ones are larger and more fleshy, have much more flavour, and can be found in a much greater variety. The little round peppers are quite common, and if you see them, do try them.

If the peppers are large, cut them lengthways into four and remove the seeds, pith and stalks.

In a saucepan large enough to take the vinegar and the peppers, bring the vinegar to the boil. Add the peppers and some salt and boil gently for 15 minutes.

Sterilise your preserving jar. Place the bay leaves on one side of the jar and fill up with the peppers and hot vinegar. Allow to cool before sealing the jar. Make sure the vinegar completely covers the peppers. Leave for a couple of months before using.

fried peppers with garlic, capers and vinegar

serves 4–6

> ❝ The most important feature of this recipe is the slightly burnt taste of the peppers (red and yellow if possible), which is obtained by frying the vegetables until the skin is scorched, or caramelised. If I was ever late coming home, I was always glad to find a dish of fried peppers in the fridge! My mother knew we would eat them cold as well. ❞

800g (1¾ lb) red and yellow sweet peppers

4 garlic cloves

1 tbsp salted capers (or capers in vinegar)

4 tbsp olive oil

2 tbsp white wine vinegar

salt to taste

Discard the seeds and cores, and cut the peppers into strips. Slice the garlic and put the salted capers to soak in a bowl of water.

Heat the oil in a large frying pan and fry the strips of pepper. The oil should be quite hot. Stir while frying, and the skins of the peppers should begin to scorch at the edges. Then add the garlic and the drained and dried capers. While these ingredients are sizzling, add the vinegar and some salt, stir well and let the vinegar evaporate for a minute. Serve immediately if you like, but it's excellent cold. (See the photograph on page 133.)

Patate Fritte con Aglio e Rosmarino

fried potatoes with garlic and rosemary

6 This simple but effective dish is a typically Italian way of cooking potatoes, making the perfect accompaniment to all kinds of roast meat. The combination of rosemary and garlic give an unmistakably Italian flavour. 9

serves 4

500g (1 lb 2 oz) potatoes, peeled weight

8 tbsp olive oil

8 large garlic cloves, unpeeled

1 sprig fresh rosemary

salt and pepper to taste

Cut the potatoes into cubes 1cm (½ in) square. Heat the olive oil in a large frying pan, and when hot add the potato cubes. Spread them well out over the pan, but do not stir-fry until they form a golden crust. Turn the potatoes over and add the garlic. Fry together to brown on all sides. Halfway through, add the rosemary leaves, salt and pepper. When the potatoes are ready, serve with the garlic. The latter will be soft and delicious, and you could squeeze it out of the skin into your mouth!

Melanzane al Funghetto
sautéed aubergines

serves 4

500g (1 lb 2 oz) aubergines

8 tbsp olive oil

2 garlic cloves, sliced

2 tbsp chopped fresh flat-leaf parsley

salt and pepper to taste

❝ "Funghetto" suggests a cooking method similar to that for preparing mushrooms, and aubergines cooked in this way really do taste a little like mushrooms. The dish is an ideal accompaniment for a veal milanese or roast chicken. ❞

Dice the aubergines. Heat the olive oil in a large frying pan and when hot add the cubed aubergine and slices of garlic. Cook over a medium heat, stirring frequently, until they look cooked. This will take about 10 minutes. Mix the parsley with the aubergines and season with salt and pepper.

Prataioli al Burro, Aglio e Prezzemolo

mushrooms with butter, garlic and parsley

6 Field mushrooms can be found everywhere, and when cooked in the following way, provide an alternative to the classic wild mushroom flavour. Try to find button mushrooms that are still closed. You can also cook other types of wild mushrooms this way, for example ceps, chanterelles, horn of plenty etc. 9

serves 4

350g (12 oz) button mushrooms

55g (2 oz) unsalted butter

1 garlic clove, chopped

3 tbsp chopped fresh flat-leaf parsley

salt and pepper to taste

If big, cut the mushrooms into three. Heat the butter until it fizzes, add the mushrooms and fry over a fierce heat until golden at the edges and all moisture has evaporated. Now add the chopped garlic, fry for only a minute, sprinkle with the parsley and season with salt and pepper. Serve immediately.

crudités with olive oil

> No one seems to know exactly where the word "pinzimonio" comes from. The dictionary says it is a derivative of the words "pinzicare" (sting) and "matrimonio" (marriage)! Whatever the truth, this is a typically Tuscan recipe that brings together good fresh vegetables, Tuscan bread and the excellent extra virgin olive oil for which Tuscany is famous. It is a spring dish, to be made around May, when asparagus, artichokes, celery, spring onions and fennel are at their best. It is an excellent way to start a meal, or is good as a simple snack.

serves 4

4 small or 2 large artichokes

8 small spring onions

2 fennel bulbs

8 tender celery stalks

16 medium asparagus spears

12 tbsp extra virgin olive oil

4 tsp salt

1 loaf unsalted Tuscan bread, or ciabatta or focaccia, sliced

Wash all the vegetables. Cut away all the tough leaves from the artichokes and trim off their tops. Slice in half, and if they are large, slice into quarters. Remove any choke. Cut the spring onions in half lengthways, if preferred. Quarter the fennel bulbs, removing any green stalks and discoloured parts. Split the celery stalks in two lengthways. Trim the asparagus.

Serve the vegetables in an earthenware dish, preferably standing in iced water. Make each person their own bowl of olive oil, with 3 tbsp oil to 1 tsp salt. Or you can serve the salt, and some pepper, separately. Dip the vegetables into the oil and seasonings, and eat with the bread (which can be toasted as bruschetta if you like).

Panzanella o Fresella
bread and tomato salad

serves 4

8 slices fresella or hard-baked granary bread (see recipe)

8 small ripe tomatoes

4 generous pinches of dried oregano

2 garlic cloves, finely chopped (optional)

4 tbsp extra virgin olive oil

salt to taste

❝ This is a typical summer dish from the region of Campania, combining a salad and a snack. The bread content is a twice-baked granary bread called "fresella", which has a delicate toasty taste. The genuine product can be found in good Italian delicatessens, or you can make it yourself at home (see below). ❞

To make your own fresella, cut thick slices of granary bread about 4cm (1½ in) thick, and bake in a preheated oven at about 160°C/325°F/Gas 3 for 15–20 minutes. They must not burn, just become crisp and completely dry. Allow to cool, and store in a dry place.

When you want to use the fresella, pass it under running cold water for a few seconds to dampen, not soak. Shake off the water and place whole on a large plate.

Chop the tomatoes and put them on top of the pieces of bread along with their juices and seeds. If you have very ripe tomatoes you can crush them directly on to the bread with your hand, as I prefer to do. Sprinkle the tomatoes with the oregano, salt and garlic (if using) and then pour the olive oil over them. Panzanella should be enjoyed with some young fresh wine.

Insalata Primaverile
spring salad

serves 6

> The spring salad, in short, should be a mixture of vegetables: obviously all the things that can be found in abundance in spring – young lettuces, both red and green, the small shoots from perennial plants in your garden such as mint, chives, parsley etc. If you cannot find these, then buy some fresh spinach. The only rule is that everything should be perfectly fresh.

85g (3 oz) radicchio

85g (3 oz) white lettuce leaves (the inner tender parts of a cos or little gem lettuce)

115g (4 oz) small spinach leaves

a small bunch of watercress

a small bunch of fresh chives

a small bunch of fresh flat-leaf parsley

2–3 sprigs fresh mint

Wash and dry all the salad ingredients very thoroughly. Slice the radicchio and lettuce into strips 1cm (½ in) wide. Leave the spinach leaves whole, but remove any long stalks. Cut the stalks off the watercress. Chop the chives into short lengths. Roughly chop the parsley and tear the mint leaves off their stalks. Choose a large bowl and mix all the leaves together in it.

Make the dressing by mixing together the olive oil and lemon juice, then season with salt and pepper. (You could use balsamic vinegar in the dressing instead of lemon juice, about 1 tbsp. But don't use the most expensive one, a ten-year-old is quite sufficient.) Only pour over the salad seconds before serving, so as to avoid the vegetables being 'cooked' by the acid in the lemon: even the freshest salad can be destroyed by being dressed too early.

Dressing

4–5 tbsp extra virgin olive oil

juice of ½ large lemon

salt and pepper to taste

tomato and celery salad

serves 4

4 large ripe tomatoes weighing 500g (1 lb 2 oz)

1 head fresh green celery

1 sweet large onion, white or red, or 5–6 large spring onions with their green stalks

1 garlic clove

6–8 fresh basil leaves, roughly torn

3 tbsp extra virgin olive oil

salt and pepper to taste

6 Summer is the season for those lovely ripe tomatoes with all the smell of the sun captured in them, and freshly picked Italian tomatoes will always be the best. Try to find plum tomatoes, or those misshapen large tomatoes, and avoid the identically shaped and sized tomatoes wrapped in plastic. 9

Skin the tomatoes by immersing them in boiling water for a few seconds, then peeling. Slice the tomatoes finely and lay them out on a large plate. Wash the celery and chop into small pieces, including the tenderest leaves. Peel and slice the onion. Chop the garlic very finely.

Lay the sliced onion over the tomatoes, and sprinkle with the chopped garlic. Scatter the celery and celery and basil leaves over the plate, and dress with the olive oil, salt and pepper. I think the tomato contains enough acid so I don't add vinegar, but if you like it go ahead.

Insalata di Fagiolini alla Menta
french bean salad with mint

serves 4

350g (12 oz) French beans, topped and tailed, or tender runner beans, trimmed and sliced

1 garlic clove

3 sprigs fresh mint

4 tbsp olive oil

juice of 1 lemon

salt and pepper to taste

❝ What could be simpler than French beans in a salad? It is important to have very fresh beans, without strings. The combination of the garlic and mint, along with the oil and lemon, gives a totally unexpected flavour. ❞

Boil the beans in plenty of salted water and cook until quite tender. Drain. Finely chop the garlic and mint. Then mix them with the oil, lemon juice, salt and pepper and stir into the beans. Mix well and eat hot or cold.

Insalata di Cavolo Verza
savoy cabbage salad

serves 4–6

1 good crisp Savoy cabbage weighing about 300g (10½ oz)

6 anchovy fillets in oil

3 tbsp white wine vinegar or balsamic vinegar

4 tbsp olive oil

salt and pepper to taste

> In winter it is difficult to find salad vegetables that haven't been greenhouse raised. The Savoy cabbage, fresh and crisp, provides an ideal alternative, and its flavour and texture make an ideal accompaniment to roast meat. I remember as a small boy stealing a beautiful cabbage from a nearby field. One friend went home with an excuse to fetch the oil, one for the anchovies, and one for the vinegar. We had found an old casserole with a broken handle. Behold, our own winter salad, eaten on a roof behind a warehouse in the chilly afternoon sun.

Peel off the darker green outside leaves of the cabbage and with a very sharp knife slice the heart as thin as you can. Avoid the stalk.

Chop the anchovies into small pieces and then in a bowl mash them together with the vinegar. When a smooth consistency, add the oil drop by drop. Season with freshly ground pepper and if necessary a little salt, but remember how salty the anchovies already are. Pour this dressing on to the cabbage, mixing well together so that every piece of cabbage is coated.

Bagna Cauda
garlic sauce with crudités

6 Bagna cauda is a typical recipe from the Piedmont region, and is usually eaten in autumn or winter when the cardoon – a common local vegetable – has had its first frost. If you can find cardoons, use them, and you could also include celeriac and Jerusalem artichokes (the cardoon and celeriac might need blanching first).

The bagna cauda is more than just a salad. It is a ceremony in which friends participate. 9

serves 6

2 red sweet peppers

2 medium artichokes

2 fennel bulbs

2 carrots

4 celery stalks

lemon juice

Sauce

10 large garlic cloves, peeled

300ml (10 fl oz) milk

10 salted anchovies, rinsed and filleted (see page 22), or 20 anchovy fillets in oil, drained

115g (4 oz) butter

4 tbsp double cream

Put the garlic cloves in a small saucepan with the milk. Bring to the boil, reduce the heat and simmer gently for 30 minutes or until the garlic is soft. Cut the anchovy fillets into small pieces and add to the garlic and milk. Cook together, stirring, and mash the anchovies with the garlic to form a paste. Add the butter in small pieces and stir until amalgamated. Remove from the heat and allow to cool a little. Sieve the mixture and then stir in the cream. Keep warm.

Wash and prepare the vegetables. Cut the red peppers lengthways into strips 1cm (½ in) wide. Remove any seeds and pith. Remove the tough leaves of the artichokes and cut off their tops. Slice each artichoke into halves and make six slices from each half, cutting away any hairy choke. Cut the fennel into halves and slice each half into six. Peel the carrots and cut each one lengthways into six long sticks. Cut the celery lengthways, each stalk into four. Fill a large bowl with ice. Squeeze a little lemon juice on the ice and arrange the vegetables on top.

Serve the bagna cauda warm in a separate bowl for each person. To keep them warm, use little table heaters.

raw cep salad

serves 4

300g (10½ oz) fresh ceps

3 tbsp extra virgin olive oil

juice of ½ lemon

1 tbsp finely chopped fresh flat-leaf parsley

salt and pepper to taste

6 Raw cultivated mushrooms make an excellent salad. However, using fresh ceps turns this sophisticated delicacy into perhaps the finest dish in the world. The ceps should be small and really fresh, and I urge you to try them despite their cost – they are incomparable. In Italy we use the Caesar's mushrooms as well, but they are relatively rare elsewhere. 9

Clean the ceps well using a brush and a knife rather than washing them, and slice thinly. Dress with oil, lemon juice, salt and pepper. Scatter the parsley over them and serve as an antipasto on slices of toast made from white bread.

I Formaggi
cheeses

The cheeses are brought to the table after il secondo, hopefully when there is a little red wine left. All sorts of cheeses are made in Italy with many regional variations. There are the famous hard cheeses such as Parmigiano Reggiano, the true Parmesan from Parma, and the more rustic pecorino, both of which are excellent eaten with fruit such as pears. Gorgonzola, the wonderful creamy blue cheese, is Lombardian and made with cows' milk. Stracchino is very soft and mild, while fontina from the Aosta valley is semi-soft and is used for fonduta, the Italian version of the Swiss fondue.

When I'm in Piedmont I love going up to Borgofranco to visit the 'balmetti', natural cellars hewn out of huge rocks where the farmers and peasants have been storing their wines in barrels for centuries. The local people go there in the late afternoon for a spuntino. Spuntino is the Italian equivalent of high tea, only instead of tea they drink wine, and instead of cucumber sandwiches they eat slices of wonderful country breads with salamis and cheeses that are hanging from the ceilings. By the end of the evening everyone is very merry and singing heartily!

Cheese is a very ancient food. The early Romans made cheese, and Roman soldiers were given a portion of cheese every day as part of their rations. Goat and sheep milks were used at first, and before the discovery of rennet, they were curdled by sharp fruit juices such as fig. Cheese is made from cows' milk in the valley of the Po, where the pastures are rich, and from goats' milk in the mountains. Sheep's milk cheese is now more common in the south and in the islands, and buffalo cheese is made from the milk of buffaloes that roam semi-wild in the swampy south. Some Italian cheeses are high in fat, others have a fat content as low as 15 per cent.

Opposite: A selection of Italian cheeses and grissini.

I Formaggi

191

hard cheeses

Parmigiano Reggiano (Parmesan)

True Parmigiano Reggiano is produced between April and November from cows' milk coming from the provinces of Bologna, Reggio, Mantova and Modena, i.e. north of the Po. Laws defining the manufacturing techniques of the cheese are very strict and a detailed description of the product must be clearly visible on the label. Only when you see this name printed on the cheese can you be sure of having bought the authentic matured product.

This cheese, one of the most famous in the world, plays an essential role in Italian cooking. It is usually grated on to various types of dishes – pasta, risotto, polenta, soups, for example – where it is used with discretion, as a seasoning. It can also be shaved on to salads, good with cold meats and some vegetables such as artichoke hearts and rocket. But it can also be eaten in chunks on its own, especially when younger, accompanied by some good bread and a glass of mature red wine. Parmesan is also excellent eaten with pears, grapes or figs as a dessert. A crumbly cheese, Parmesan contains only 28–32 per cent fat, and is high in protein. It is also very digestible, and is recommended for invalids and children in Italy. It should never thicken, curdle or go stringy when it is added to hot food; if it sinks to the bottom of the plate, it is not the real thing.

Parmesan belongs to the 'grana' (meaning 'grain') family, grana being the generic name for all Italian fine-textured hard cheeses which originated in the valley of the Po. Grana padano is a similar but slightly inferior cheese, industrially manufactured from milk coming from different regions outside the area where Parmigiano Reggiano is made. It is less matured than the real Parmesan, and therefore damper in consistency. I suggest you buy this type only when you can't obtain the true Reggiano type.

Both cheeses are made in huge circular shapes weighing 30–40kg (66–88lb) and matured for at least eighteen months (and up to four years in the case of some Parmesans). A very young Parmesan called 'giovane' is sold after fourteen months, a 'vecchio' after eighteen months to two years, a 'stravecchio' after two to three years, and a 'stravecchione' after three to four years. (In some famous restaurants in Italy, minestrone is served in the hollowed-out rinds of Parmesan cheeses: as the soup is served, the sides are scraped with a ladle, and some of the cheese is dissolved into the soup.)

Always buy both Parmesan and grana padano by the piece and grate it when you need it. Keep in the fridge wrapped in a damp cloth. Never ever buy the pre-grated variety, as the essential flavour of the cheese will have completely evaporated. And don't ever throw away the rind of a piece of Parmesan that you have finished: put it into a soup like minestrone, and it will still give out plenty of flavour.

Pecorino

Pecorino may be sold fresh, medium or mature. The fresh (sometimes called 'caciotta') does not keep, but the matured pecorino, which keeps for some months, is used in much the same way as Parmesan, grated on pasta and other dishes.

Pecorino is made from sheep's milk, 'pecora', from which it takes its name, in golden yellow wheel shapes with rush or straw markings, weighing about 2kg (4½ lb). It comes from central and southern Italy and two islands, Sicily and Sardinia. The two regions which both produce and use the most pecorino are Lazio (where they call the cheese pecorino romano) and Sardinia (where they call it pecorino sardo). The further south you go, the spicier the pecorino becomes. The Tuscan version produced in Pienza (pecorino toscano), is sweet and mature, while some Sicilian and Calabrian ones can contain whole peppercorns and are very spicy as a result. (I once saw some Sardinians devouring a very well-matured pecorino which seemed perfect except for the fact that it was crawling with maggots. Apparently this was considered a special delicacy!). The rind of pecorino cheeses varies according to the wishes of the producer and the habits of the area: pecorino romano, for instance, is rubbed with oil and wood ash.

Roman pecorino is probably the oldest cheese produced in Italy, and it was served on the tables of rich and poor alike. It is similar to the Sardinian pecorino – pale, almost grey in colour, and nearly always made in the characteristic round rush baskets and then air-dried. In Sicily the pecorino siciliano is often called 'canestrato', after the baskets.

The Romans love to eat fresh pecorino together with very young broad beans and good bread.

Ricotta salata

This is usually a derivative of pecorino, being made from its whey and then dried, although it can also be made from goats' milk. It comes mainly from the south and is used grated on pasta. The flavour is similar to that of pecorino, but it is much less fatty.

Provolone

The enormous pear-shaped cheeses which hang from strings in Italian food shops, and look as if they are covered in wax,

are provoloni. They come from the south of Italy and are produced in various sizes and flavours – and indeed shapes (from cottage loaves to torpedoes). The one most popular in the north is made from cows' milk with calf's rennet, is sweet-tasting and usually sold fresh, or no more than two to three months old. The cheese made with goats' (or lambs') rennet, is spicy and suitable for maturing – the more matured it is, the spicier and harder it becomes – and is preferred by people from the south.

The cheese contains 45 per cent fat.

Caciocavallo

This cheese takes its name (literally 'horse cheese') from the way it is hung to dry and mature – two cheeses strung together on 'horseback' over a pole. It is common in the south of Italy, as well as in the Balkans and in Hungary. Made from cows' milk sometimes mixed with goats' milk, its layered texture is similar to that of provolone, and its shape varies from oval to square. It has a pleasantly spicy taste if matured, and is sweet when fresh. It is eaten in slices or grated on some pasta dishes.

Toma

Piedmont is famous for its toma, which is made from cows' milk in nearly every valley in the region. Each cheese usually weighs 2–3kg (4½–6½ lb) and is sold in various stages of maturity, the maximum being about two years. Most of the consumption of toma is local.

Eaten fresh as a dessert cheese, toma has names like paglierina, tomella and tomini. (Caprini is similar, but made with goats' milk.)

semi-soft cheeses

These cheeses are found all over the north of Italy. During the summer months the herds of cows stay up on the high mountains where they graze on sweet aromatic alpine grass. This is what gives the region's cheese and butter their distinctive taste. In autumn there are never-ending processions of animals being brought down to the valleys for the winter. The cowbells round their necks clatter noisily and they are led by a festival queen, followed by her page – the youngest calf, wearing a tricolour scarf.

Fontina

Fontina is made exclusively in the Val d'Aosta region, and was once made with sheep's milk. The genuine cheese bears a proper mark of quality with the inscription 'Fontina from the Val d'Aosta'. There are many imitations, but their quality and flavour do not come anywhere near the original, which is pale creamy yellow in colour and has a definite nutty sweetness. Fontina is particularly good for cooking fonduta, the Italian version of fondue, as it melts so well, and is delicious eaten with good fresh bread.

Each cheese is round and flat, weighs up to 15–20 kg (33–44 lb) and has a thin reddish brown rind. It contains 45 per cent fat.

Bel Paese

Translated literally, 'bel paese' means 'beautiful country'. It was developed and named in the early twentieth century by the Galbani family to celebrate Italy, which is why the typical silhouette of Italy is imprinted on the cheese. The cheeses weigh 2kg (4½ lb), but you can find a very small version, about the size of a hamburger, to be taken on picnics.

Both cheeses are wrapped in wax to maintain their freshness. Bel Paese is very creamy in texture, mild in flavour and pale cream in colour.

Bel Paese is made from cows' milk, and has a 45–52 per cent fat content. It can be eaten on its own or, as it melts easily, used in cooking.

Asiago

A cows' milk cheese from the Veneto region made in the high plain of Asiago near Vicenza. (Sheep, not cows, were once the source of milk.) Asiago d'allevo is made from semi-skimmed milk, and has a fat content of only 30 per cent. Asiago pressato is made from pasteurised full-cream milk, thus its fat content is higher, at around 45 per cent. The cheeses, large flat wheels, weigh about 10kg (22 lb) each, and are matured for from two to eighteen months, depending on type, becoming spicier and harder with age. Asiago d'allevo, which can be matured for twelve to eighteen months, is suitable for grating.

The cheeses have a greyish-yellow rind, and the straw-coloured paste has lots of small eyes. They can be eaten on their own and used for cooking.

Provola, Provolini, Burrini and Ciccillo

All of these cheeses are very similar: they have a fresh, creamy provolone base and are pear-shaped. Burrini are provola cheeses with unsalted butter in the middle; this gives a particular sweetness to the cheese, which is usually eaten on its own. It is made locally in the south of Italy. Each cheese weighs about 500g (1 lb 2 oz), and is characteristically tied with a blade of straw.

soft cheeses

Stracchino, Crescenza and Robiola

At one time the group of cheeses known as stracchino – which includes Gorgonzola – was made almost exclusively from the milk of cows fed on hay in wintertime when they had come down from their alpine pastures. Stracchino (see below), for example, takes its name from the word 'stracchi' which in the dialects of Piedmont and Lombardy means 'tired' – perhaps indicating how the cows felt after the long journey back down to the valleys. A defining characteristic of stracchino cheeses is that they are made from still warm milk, which includes some of the milk from the day before. In parts of northern Italy, robiola, for instance, can be made from sheep's and goats' milk as well as cows'. Originally the cheeses were made in winter when the cold conditions enabled them to be stored for a while. Nowadays, of course, this is not a problem and they are available the whole year round. They are very soft rindless cheeses and are sold in specially wrapped portions ranging from 115g (4 oz) or more to 2–4kg (4½–9 lb) in weight. Their flavour is deliciously fresh and sweet with a slight hint of sharpness. These typical dessert cheeses reach maturity in ten days, and can be spread on bread or biscuits, but have few uses in cooking.

Taleggio

Another cheese typical of northern Italy, which has been made in Lombardy, some say, since the eleventh century. The cheeses are about 20cm (8 in) square, weigh about 2kg (4½ lb), and are wrapped in a special paper to maintain freshness. Taleggio has a 48 per cent fat content, a soft sweet flavour and creamy texture. It reaches maturity after only about six to eight weeks, and is an ideal dessert cheese. I also use it to cook with, as it does not go stringy.

Gorgonzola and the Veined Cheeses

Gorgonzola is made from a base of cows' milk stracchino with the addition of the harmless fungus *Penicillium glaucum* which transforms it into the unique Italian blue cheese. Until the twentieth century, it was known as stracchino verde, but then it took the name of its place of origin, which is near Milan. It is now made all over Italy. It has a 48 per cent fat content and a strong buttery taste and texture. The cheeses are made in large shapes weighing about 4–6kg (9–13½ lb).

There are several variations. Apart from the sweet Gorgonzola, there is a spicier, more mature one. The other erborinati – all the green- or blue-veined cheeses – are castelmagno, made in the province of Cuneo in Piedmont; dolce verde which is sold in tubes; dolcelatte, which is a milder and creamier version of Gorgonzola (which, although famous, does not have an official denomination); and torta di san gaudenzio, made of alternating layers of Gorgonzola and mascarpone.

Gorgonzola has various uses, particularly as a dessert cheese, and is delicious in sauces for fennel, pasta, gnocchi and polenta.

fresh cheeses

Mascarpone

This must be the fattiest cheese on earth: it contains 80 per cent fat. In fact it's not a true cheese at all, in that no rennet is used in its creation; instead it is made from an extremely rich cream, and whipped to an almost solid but very velvety consistency. Because it has a neutral taste it is used almost exclusively for making desserts – see page 209 – and sweet sauces, although it can be used in a savoury context as well.

Ricotta

After Parmesan, ricotta is the cheese most frequently used in cooking. However, like mascarpone, it is not a true cheese, rather a by-product of cheese-making, being made from the whey after its separation from the curd. (One of the most famous Italian ricotti is made from the whey of the sheep's milk used in the manufacture of pecorino.)

Ricotta can be made with cows' and sheep's milk as well as that of goats, or from a mixture; the fat content varies according to the milk used, but is usually between 15 and 20 per cent. One exception is when the ricotta has been made with buffalo milk that has been used to produce mozzarella. This consequently has a much higher fat content. Ricotta is used in many cooked dishes and pasta fillings. It is widely used in desserts and cakes as well.

There is also a semi-fresh ricotta that is eaten as a dessert cheese, and ricotta salata, mentioned on page 193.

When you are buying ricotta, use it as soon as possible, because it quickly becomes acid.

Mozzarella

This versatile cheese, used in many dishes for its astounding melting quality, was originally made only from buffalo milk. It was produced mainly in the south, on the plain of Aversa and in the area near Rome called the Agro Pontino. (The buffaloes are said to have been introduced from India in the sixteenth century.) The original version is kneaded by hand while the whey is still very hot (a process that gives the cheese its characteristic 'layered' appearance), and is much more expensive than the factory-made type produced in the north of Italy from cows' milk.

Various types of mozzarella exist, including walnut-sized bocconcini, 'pleats' of varying sizes, and the classic round mozzarella which weighs about 200g (7 oz). Good mozzarella should be very white and fairly elastic, and still be moist when sliced (the freshness can be gauged by the 'tears' of whey that emerge). The cows' milk version is decidedly more rubbery in texture.

When mozzarella is cooked it melts and goes very stringy. For this reason it is an essential ingredient in pizza, and many baked dishes such as *La Parmigiana di Melanzane* (although I tend to use fontina instead, see page 154). But mostly mozzarella is eaten in its natural state, uncooked and seasoned with salt, pepper and a trickle of extra virgin olive oil (walnut oil is good too), or in a salad with tomatoes and basil.

Mozzarella's popularity has grown enormously outside Italy over the last few years, and it is now often produced by non-Italian companies. Avoid at all costs the hard blocks made in Denmark and Belgium which bear no resemblance to genuine mozzarella. The Italian type is exported in plastic bags which contain some liquid to keep them fresh.

Smoked mozzarella can be found in good delicatessens. Brownish in colour, it is mostly eaten raw as an antipasto.

Fonduta con Tartufi
fondue with truffle

6 A classic Piedmontese dish featuring the excellent fontina cheese from the Val d'Aosta with those jewels of nature – white Alba truffles. A fonduta with truffles is sheer delight, but it can also be eaten just by itself. 9

serves 4

400g (14 oz) fontina cheese

300ml (10 fl oz) milk

8 medium egg yolks

30g (a good 1 oz) unsalted butter

1 small white truffle (optional)

Cut the fontina into very small cubes and leave to soak in the milk for at least 4 hours. The milk should just cover the cheese. Thoroughly beat the eggs.

Melt the butter in the top of a double boiler (or a small pan over simmering water), then add the beaten egg yolks, the cheese and a little of the milk that hasn't been absorbed by the cheese. Melt together over a very gentle heat, stirring all the time, until the cheese and eggs have amalgamated into a thick, but not separated, cream. Pour into a heated earthenware bowl and serve at once, adding thinly sliced truffle if you like. Eat with bread or croûtons, which you dip into the cheese sauce as you would with Swiss fondue.

Mozzarella in Carrozza
deep-fried mozzarella

serves 4

8 slices thin white bread

200g (7 oz) fresh mozzarella

2 eggs

125ml (4 fl oz) milk

6 tbsp plain flour

olive oil for deep- or shallow-frying

salt and pepper to taste

6 The imagination of the Neapolitans has gone so far as to put the mozzarella in a "carrozza" (carriage), one of the symbols of old Naples. It is a very easy, tasty recipe if cooked with a good stringy mozzarella and eaten right away. It can be served as a first or main course, along with a green salad. 9

Cut the crusts off the bread so that each slice measures 10 x 6cm (4 x 2½ in). Slice the mozzarella into 4 thick slices about 1cm (½ in) thick. Beat the eggs lightly and season with salt and pepper. Dip the slices of bread on one side into the milk and then place a slice of mozzarella on the dry side. Season the mozzarella with salt and pepper and make a sandwich with another slice of bread, milk-soaked side on the outside. Dust the sandwich with flour and then soak in the beaten egg.

Heat the oil in a deep-fryer; alternatively heat oil about 2cm (¾ in) deep in a pan. Fry the sandwich in the hot oil, turning it over if you are shallow-frying. The sandwich should be a nice golden colour, slightly crisp on the outside and the mozzarella filling should have begun to melt on the inside. Drain on kitchen paper and serve immediately.

Mozzarella Affumicata Fritta
fried smoked mozzarella

serves 4

1 smoked mozzarella weighing about 250g (9 oz)

3 tbsp plain flour

1 egg, beaten

4 tbsp dry breadcrumbs

55g (2 oz) butter

6 Smoked mozzarella, with its brownish smoky-flavoured skin and firm texture, is delicious in salads. This recipe makes a tasty antipasto or snack. 9

Slice the mozzarella into four thick slices. Dust each slice with flour, dip into the beaten egg and then coat with the breadcrumbs. Heat the butter in a heavy pan until it fizzes. Fry the mozzarella slices until crisp and brown on each side. It will take less than a minute to seal the coating. The cheese should hardly have melted or the slices will fall apart. Serve with a lettuce or rocket salad.

La Frutta e i Dolci
fruit and desserts

When I was a child, it was my job to buy the fruit every day. As soon as I got home from school, I'd get on my bike and go off to choose fruit freshly picked from the trees. We would usually eat everything I bought that day. If there was any fruit left over, it was stewed or made into preserves. Still today, most Italians will finish their meals with a piece of ripe seasonal fruit.

Wonderful fruit sorbets, ice-creams and granitas are included in a meal or eaten at cafés in the heat of the day. The Italians are famous for their frozen desserts, and these were developed through the Arab invasion of Sicily (the influences of which are still apparent in many aspects of Sicilian cuisine). The Arabs gathered ice from the slopes of Mount Etna and stored it in caves. The ice crystals were then mixed with sweet fruit syrups, to make what we now call sorbets. Ice-cream, made with cream and flavourings, was developed later.

Although special desserts, rich in starch and cream, are generally reserved for special occasions, such as birthdays and Christmas, there are some superb Italian recipes – fruit tarts, baked peaches, pears in wine, puddings made of ricotta cheese, mascarpone eaten with stewed fruits. Certain Italian specialities have become popular abroad in recent years, among them zabaglione. Pannacotta, too, is popular, a set cream with vanilla, and tiramisú. Some sweets and cakes are served only at Christmas or Easter – pastiera di napoli is made at Easter, for example, while struffoli di napoli, cannoli alla siciliana and panettone di milano are all symbolic of Christmas. Italians are big eaters of biscuits, especially for breakfast, dipped in coffee, or enjoyed with a sweet wine.

Opposite: *Pere Cotte al Forno* (see page 208).

strawberries with balsamic vinegar and pepper

serves 4

500g (1 lb 2 oz) strawberries, hulled and halved

30g (a good 1 oz) caster sugar

1 tbsp balsamic vinegar

freshly ground black pepper

6 In Italy we eat a great deal of soft fruit such as strawberries, blackberries, mulberries and blueberries. However, we never generally combine these fruits with cream, but with ingredients that enhance their flavour. For instance, adding a few drops of lemon juice and some sugar is the most common way to eat soft fruit. But a new idea is to sprinkle on a few drops of balsamic vinegar, and then some freshly ground black pepper. It sounds bizarre, but I can tell you that it's delicious, a completely new sensation! 9

Put the strawberries into a big stainless-steel or ceramic bowl. Add the sugar and vinegar and toss well to coat all the strawberries. Chill and serve in individual bowls with a twist of black pepper.

baked stuffed peaches

serves 4

6 A typical recipe from Piedmont where peaches grow in abundance. You will need those lovely big ripe peaches with the yellow or white flesh (or you could use nectarines). This dish can be made well in advance as baked peaches are excellent cold, but not straight from the fridge. 9

4 ripe yellow or white peaches

2 tbsp unsweetened cocoa powder

4 macaroon biscuits (amaretti), crumbled

2 egg yolks

3 tbsp caster sugar, plus 2–3 drops vanilla essence, or 2 tbsp vanilla sugar

1 tbsp pine nuts

100ml (3½ fl oz) whipping cream

Preheat the oven to 200°C/400°F/Gas 6.

Cut the peaches in two and remove the stones. Scoop out some of the flesh from the middle of the peaches to make room for the filling. Mix the cocoa with the biscuits, egg yolks, 2 tbsp of the sugar, the vanilla and pine nuts, blending well. Fill the cavities of the peaches with this mixture.

Grease an ovenproof dish and put the peaches in it. Bake in the preheated oven for 15–20 minutes. Before serving, hot or cold, whip the cream with the remaining sugar, and serve next to the peach.

This excellent dessert needs a nice glass of Moscato d'Asti to go with it.

quinces in syrup

> ❛ Quinces have a very distinctive flavour, but are good only when cooked. Quince jam and jelly are both delicious, and an apple pie or tart is transformed when a few slices of quince are included. An easy way to cook quinces as a dessert is to stew them in water and sugar which will become syrupy after the cooking. ❜

serves 6

4 large quinces or 1kg (2¼ lb) smaller ones

200g (7 oz) caster sugar

rind and juice of 1 lemon

1 cinnamon stick, 10cm (4 in) long

10 cloves

Peel, core and slice the quinces thinly. Put in a pan with the sugar, lemon rind and juice and the spices. Pour in enough water to cover, and simmer on a moderate heat until cooked, about an hour. Remove the quinces from the pan and boil the liquid rapidly to reduce it to a syrup. Strain, pour over the quinces and serve cold.

Crostata di Lamponi
raspberry tart

> Italians love fruit or jam tarts, and they call them "crostati", named after the crisp pastry. When using fresh raw fruit, the pastry case is blind baked first, as here, but many tarts are made with raw pastry and a fruit jam filling, when both are cooked together.

serves 6–8

700g (1 lb 9 oz) fresh raspberries

125ml (4 fl oz) water

juice of 1 lemon

150g (5½ oz) caster sugar

4 gelatine leaves (or equivalent amount of powdered gelatine)

1 tbsp icing sugar

Pastry

250g (9 oz) plain flour

55g (2 oz) caster sugar

a pinch of salt

115g (4 oz) unsalted butter

4 tbsp dry sherry

This tart is wonderful when made with freshly gathered wild raspberries. Alternatively, any fruits such as blueberries, blackberries and strawberries can be used.

To make the pastry, sieve together the flour, sugar and salt, then add the butter cut into small pieces. Mix together with your fingertips until the texture is like breadcrumbs. Add the sherry and mix lightly to make a dough. Cover and put aside in a cool place for at least an hour.

Preheat the oven to 180°C/350°F/Gas 4.

Roll out the pastry and line a tart tin 25cm (10 in) in diameter. Prick the surface with a fork and bake in the preheated oven for 15–20 minutes or until the pastry is cooked.

Wash the raspberries if necessary, and choose 175g (6 oz) of the least good-looking ones. Put them in a small saucepan with the water, half the lemon juice, and the sugar. Boil until the juice becomes slightly syrupy. Remove from the heat, stir in the gelatine and leave to cool a little. Meanwhile, sprinkle the remaining raspberries with a little of the remaining lemon juice.

When the pastry and the raspberry syrup have cooled, spread a layer of the jellied syrup over the bottom of the pastry case. Arrange the fresh raspberries on top, next to each other in a decorative way to make concentric circles. Leave to set before serving, and sprinkle with just a little icing sugar.

campari and passionfruit sorbet

serves 10

> ❝ Campari is probably the best-known Italian aperitif the world over. With its intense red colour and its sophisticated bitter taste, produced by the infusion of various herbs, it can be used in cocktails as well as drunk by itself. Combined with the intense flavour of passionfruit, the result is deeply exotic. (I admit passionfruit don't grow in Italy, but I've made this one exception!) I created this sorbet many years ago, and it has become a much appreciated, refreshing finale to a meal. ❞

1kg (2¼ lb) passionfruit

100ml (3½ fl oz) Campari

1 litre (1¾ pints) water

500g (1 lb 2 oz) caster sugar

250g (9 oz) glucose

mint leaves (optional), for decoration

Halve the passionfruit, and scrape the flesh and seeds out into a sieve over a bowl. Push the flesh through so that as much juice as possible is obtained, while the black seeds are left behind.

Mix everything except the mint together, and put into a sorbet machine. Churn until a smooth consistency and it is frozen, then place in the freezer.

Before serving, remove from the freezer and leave to soften for 10 minutes. Scoop into balls and serve in frosted glasses or other dishes, topped with mint leaves if you like. A biscuit, such as that on page 214, would be a good accompaniment.

Pere Cotte al Forno
pears baked in red wine

> ❮ Another very easily prepared recipe using cooked pears, which can be found in many Italian restaurants. My mother used to make it in autumn when pears are plentiful and when the first wine has just been pressed. She would always make more than was needed; apart from being a dessert, it was also something special for us when we returned ravenous from school. The alcohol in the wine disappears when cooked, so the pears can be given to children. ❯

serves 10

10 Conference pears

1.2 litres (2 pints) dry red wine

1 cinnamon stick, 5cm (2 in) long

a few cloves

rind of 1 lemon, cut into strips

300g (10½ oz) caster sugar

Wash the pears and pack tightly, side by side, in a deep-sided ovenproof dish. Pour the wine over and add the cinnamon, cloves and lemon rind, then sprinkle half the sugar on the pears. Put into a cold oven and bring the temperature up to 200°C/400°F/Gas 6. Cook, basting the pears every now and then with the juices. After 45 minutes sprinkle the remaining sugar on to the pears and cook for a final 10 minutes. Leave to cool before serving.

If too much liquid remains, reduce it a little by boiling it, then pour it over the pears before leaving them to cool. The pears are best served with a scoop of good vanilla ice-cream. (See the photograph on page 201.)

Tiramisú
pick-me-up

serves 4

> This is one of my favourite desserts, made with that killer of a cheese, mascarpone. There are many recipes for tiramisú, which translated means "pick-me-up" or "lift-me-up", due obviously to the large amount of calories – and caffeine! – in it. This recipe is my version of the original.

1 egg yolk

1 tbsp caster sugar

1 tsp vanilla sugar

250g (9 oz) mascarpone cheese

175ml (6 fl oz) strong black coffee

1 tbsp coffee liqueur (Kahlua)

10–12 Savoiardi biscuits

1–2 tbsp unsweetened cocoa powder

Put the egg, sugar and vanilla sugar in a bowl and mix gently to a creamy consistency. Add the mascarpone and fold in to obtain a cream.

Put the coffee in a bowl with the coffee liqueur. Dip the biscuits for a second or two in the coffee mixture, letting them absorb just enough to keep firm but not fall apart. Starting with the biscuits, arrange in four individual dishes alternating layers of biscuit and mascarpone, ending with mascarpone. Dust with cocoa powder and put into the fridge to set and chill.

ricotta tart

> ❝ This tart is another cheese-based dessert which my mother used to make from time to time as a special treat, usually on a Sunday. Ricotta is used all over Italy to make sweets. However, the method and ingredients, primarily the use of citrus peel, suggest that this recipe comes from the south. ❞

serves 10

1 recipe *Pastry* (see page 205)

Filling

45g (1½ oz) each of candied orange peel, candied lemon peel and angelica

45g (1½ oz) bitter dessert chocolate

2 egg yolks

150g (5½ oz) caster sugar

rind of ½ lemon, very finely chopped

500g (1 lb 2 oz) very fresh ricotta cheese

Make the pastry as described on page 205, then cover and put aside in a cool place for at least an hour.

The candied peel, angelica and chocolate should all be chopped into very small pieces, about 5mm (¼ in) square. Beat the egg yolks with the sugar until creamy, then add the chopped lemon zest. Beat the ricotta with a fork until light, then add it to the egg mixture. Finally, stir in the candied peel and chocolate pieces.

Preheat the oven to 190°C/375°F/Gas 5. Line the bottom and sides of a cake tin with three-quarters of the pastry. Pour in the ricotta mixture and spread it evenly. Roll out the rest of the pastry and cut into strips 2cm (¾ in) wide. Make a lattice top on the tart. Put in the preheated oven and bake until the top starts to turn brown, about 30–40 minutes. Serve cold.

Cannoli alla Siciliana
sicilian cannoli

> 6 This is a very typical Sicilian speciality using, once again, ricotta cheese. To shape the cannoli, you need four or five cylinders 2.5cm (1 in) in diameter and 15cm (6 in) long. In Italy they use lengths of bamboo cane, and they also sell the equivalent in tin. 9

makes 24 cannoli

Pastry

25g (1 oz) butter

25g (1 oz) caster sugar

1 large egg

3½ tbsp dry white wine

2 tbsp vanilla sugar

a pinch of salt

150g (5½ oz) plain flour

To finish

1 egg, beaten

plenty of lard for deep-frying

icing sugar for dusting

Filling

500g (1 lb 2 oz) very fresh ricotta cheese

115g (4 oz) caster sugar

1 tbsp vanilla sugar

2 tbsp orange-flower water

55g (2 oz) each of glacé cherries, angelica, candied lemon peel and candied orange peel, very finely chopped

85g (3 oz) plain dessert chocolate, in tiny pieces

For the pastry, beat the butter, sugar and egg together until light and creamy. Add the wine, vanilla sugar and salt and mix together. Fold in the flour and knead a bit to form a dough. Put the dough aside in a cool place for at least 2 hours.

Roll out the dough with a rolling pin to a large sheet 5mm (¼ in) thick. Cut the sheet into 12cm (5 in) squares. Place a bamboo cane diagonally across the square of pastry and wrap the two opposite corners around the cane to form each cannolo. Seal the join by wetting the pastry with beaten egg. Make three or four at a time if you can.

Now heat the lard in a large deep pan: it must be deep enough to cover the cannoli. When very hot, carefully put the cannoli in to fry. I find a long-pronged cooking fork is the best implement for handling the cannoli. They are cooked when they are golden brown, about 1½–2 minutes. The pastry will puff up as it cooks, so the cannoli have a plump tube shape. Drain on kitchen paper. Only remove the metal tubes or bamboo cane when the cannoli are cool.

To make the filling, beat the ricotta cheese with a fork, then add the sugar, vanilla sugar and orange-flower water. The ricotta should become creamier in consistency. Mix the remaining ingredients into the ricotta. Fill each cannoli with the ricotta mixture and line up on a plate. Dust with icing sugar and serve cool, but do not refrigerate.

wheat tart

serves 10 or more

> In Naples, Easter isn't Easter without this wonderful tart. It has, apparently, very ancient origins, and it symbolises wealth. Grain and ricotta cheese are the most basic of foods, and if you do not have them, it means you are very poor. Whatever Neapolitans may think of this, the tart is still a remarkable sweet. The important ingredient for it is whole-wheat grain, which is available in good health-food shops. Allow plenty of time for preparation.

Pastry

150g (5½ oz) caster sugar

150g (5½ oz) butter or cooking fat

3 large egg yolks

300g (10½ oz) plain flour

Filling

200g (7 oz) whole wheat, soaked in water for 24 hours, and cooked the day before, or a 440g (15½ oz) can cooked wheat

600ml (1 pint) milk (if you are using fresh wheat)

finely grated zest of ½ lemon and ½ orange

1 tsp ground cinnamon

2 tsp vanilla sugar

300g (10½ oz) ricotta cheese

4 large eggs, separated

2 tbsp orange-flower water

150g (5½ oz) candied peel, finely diced

225g (8 oz) caster sugar

icing sugar for dusting

Simmer the soaked fresh grain in the milk with the lemon zest for 3–4 hours on a very low heat. Depending on the grain it may absorb more or less milk. If too wet, drain off some milk. When cooked, add the cinnamon, vanilla sugar and orange zest. Cool and keep until the next day. Alternatively, use the canned ready-cooked grain and add to it the same ingredients.

For the pastry work together the sugar, butter and egg yolks, then add the flour and make a smooth pastry. Chill.

Preheat the oven to 190°C/375°F/Gas 5.

Beat the ricotta with the egg yolks and the orange-flower water. Add the candied peel and the wheat. Beat the egg whites with the caster sugar and fold very gently into the ricotta.

Butter a large flan tin 35cm (14 in) in diameter. Press two-thirds of the pastry into it, covering the bottom and sides. Pour in the filling. Roll out the remaining pastry and cut into long strips to form a lattice top. Bake for about 45 minutes. Allow to cool, and dust with icing sugar.

granny's lies

serves 6

> 6 A granny shouldn't tell lies, but these particular ones are sweet lies – made from strips of pastry that are then cut into ribbons and tied in bows by a patient granny. They can be eaten after an informal dinner, or in the afternoon, with a cup of coffee. Like cannoli, they are best fried in lard. 9

55g (2 oz) butter

250g (9 oz) plain flour

1 large egg, beaten

2 tbsp granulated sugar

a pinch of salt

5 tbsp sweet vermouth

lard or olive oil for deep-frying

icing sugar for dusting

Mix the butter with the flour, as for pastry, until the texture is like breadcrumbs. Add the egg, sugar, salt and finally the vermouth. Knead to a smooth dough. This takes 5 minutes or so, and the dough should be fairly stiff. Alternatively, use an electric mixer with a blade for dough-making. Put the dough to rest in a cool place for 2 hours or more.

To make the busie, roll out the dough to a thickness of 3mm (⅛ in). If you have a pasta machine, you can use it to roll the dough out into long strips of the right thickness. With a jagged pastry wheel, cut the dough into strips 2.5cm (1 in) wide and 20cm (8 in) long. Gently tie the strips into bows.

Heat the lard in a large deep pan and when it is very hot, fry the bows two or three at a time until golden brown. Remove, drain on kitchen paper and allow to cool. Pile them up and sprinkle with icing sugar.

Biscotti di Meliga
polenta biscuits

makes 30–40 biscuits

300g (10½ oz) maize flour
(polenta, instant or quick-cook)

110g (scant 4 oz) plain flour

a pinch of salt

200g (7 oz) unsalted butter, plus
extra for greasing

finely grated zest of ½ lemon

2 medium eggs, plus 1 egg yolk

200g (7 oz) granulated sugar

6 "Meliga" is the Piedmontese name for maize flour from which polenta is usually made. Maize flour is very common in Italy – and is becoming more familiar here now – and one way to use it is in the making of desserts. For this recipe you will need the instant or quick-cook maize flour that can be found in any good Italian delicatessen. These biscuits are usually found in Carmagnola, near Turin, and also in the Aosta valley. 9

Preheat the oven to 190°C/375°F/Gas 5.

Combine the polenta with the flour and salt, then add the butter, cut up into small pieces, and the lemon zest. Mix together to a soft breadcrumb consistency using your finger-tips. Beat the eggs and sugar together and then mix into the flour and butter to obtain a soft sticky dough.

Butter a large flat baking tin. Using a piping bag with a large nozzle, 1cm (½ in) in diameter, squeeze out 'S' shapes, circles and dots. Don't put them too close to each other as they will spread a little when cooking. Bake in the preheated oven for 15 minutes. The biscuits should be a wonderful gold colour with a darker brown rim. They are very crumbly and delicious. (See the photograph on page 207.)

Fritole di Lino
angels' farts

serves 6–8

> 6 We were celebrating my wife's birthday at La Trattoria da Lino in Soligheto, near Treviso, when our host produced an enormous heap of these puffs. They were so perfectly delicious that we ate every one. It seemed to me that there was only one way to describe their heavenly lightness – and now our name for them is "angels' farts". 9

125ml (4 fl oz) milk

125ml (4 fl oz) water

55g (2 oz) granulated sugar

15g (½ oz) unsalted butter

a pinch of salt

200g (7 oz) plain flour

2 tsp Lievito Bertolini (baking powder with vanilla, available in Italian delicatessens)

4 medium eggs

olive oil for deep-frying

icing sugar for sprinkling

Put the milk, water, sugar, butter and salt into a saucepan and bring to the boil. Sift in the flour and baking powder and stir briefly: the mixture will become very stiff. Remove from the heat and allow to cool, then knead in the eggs, one by one.

Fill a pan with olive oil about 2cm (¾ in) deep, and heat until hot. Drop in a tsp of dough. The dough will almost immediately start to swell, becoming perfectly round. Surprisingly, it turns itself over in the hot oil so as to gently brown on all sides. The balls of dough will increase four times in size during cooking. Remove from the oil and put aside to drain, but keep warm. When you have discovered how these balls grow, fry them two or three at a time, according to the size of your pan. Don't let the oil get too hot: the slow puffing up of the dough, which takes about 2 minutes, is essential to their lightness. When biting into the fritters, the outside should be crisp and the inside practically hollow.

To make the zabaglione, follow the recipe on page 216.

Make a small incision in your fritter balls and push a tsp of zabaglione into the hollow. You could pipe the zabaglione in, using a piping bag. Sprinkle with icing sugar, and serve hot.

Zabaglione

4 large egg yolks

100g (3½ oz) caster sugar

150ml (5 fl oz) Marsala

Zabaglione al Moscato
zabaglione with muscatel

serves 4

4 medium egg yolks

110g (scant 4 oz) caster sugar

175ml (6 fl oz) Moscato Passito

6 Zabaglione is one of the best-known Italian desserts, and it is eaten by itself or used as a filling (see page 215). You will find this delicious recipe, based on eggs, in nearly every Italian restaurant, both in Italy and abroad. Marsala wine is normally used along with sugar to produce the fluffy consistency. The use of a good dessert wine such as Moscato Passito instead of Marsala gives it a fresh fragrance. If you don't have a special copper pan or bain-marie, you can use a round bowl standing in a large pan of hot water. 9

Beat the egg yolks with the sugar until the sugar is dissolved. Add the wine and beat for a few minutes more. Put in the bain-marie over a low heat and, using a whisk, beat until a firm, foamy consistency is obtained. This will take about 5–10 minutes, depending on the freshness of the eggs and on the heat. Take care not to overcook it and turn it into scrambled eggs! Pour into individual glasses and serve with very delicately flavoured biscuits.

Struffoli di Napoli
neapolitan struffoli

serves 10

5 medium eggs

3 tbsp granulated sugar

500g (1 lb 2 oz) plain flour

finely grated zest of 1 lemon
and 1 orange

a pinch of salt

1 tbsp pure alcohol
(if unavailable, strong vodka
will do)

olive oil for deep-frying

Caramel

110g (scant 4 oz) caster sugar

250g (9 oz) honey

2 tbsp water

Decoration

55g (2 oz) angelica,
finely chopped

25g (1 oz) silver balls

6 If Naples can't celebrate Easter without its pastiera, then it is even more unthinkable to celebrate Christmas without struffoli. These little sweets are an absolute must. My mother used to make them for Christmas and they were enthusiastically devoured by all of us. In many families they will be made as presents for friends and relatives. 9

To make the dough, beat the eggs with the sugar, then mix in the flour, adding the lemon and orange zest, salt and alcohol. Knead well for 3–4 minutes, make into a ball and cover. Leave to rest for 2 hours in a cool place.

Take a little bit of dough at a time and roll into sausage shapes with your hand to a diameter of 1cm (½ in). Cut the sausage into small pieces 1cm (½ in) long. It is quite laborious rolling out these sausages and will take you some time.

Heat the oil in a small pan so that the oil is 2–3cm (about 1 in) deep. Fry the struffoli quite a few at a time in the hot oil until slightly brown, remove and drain on kitchen paper. Continue this way until all the dough is used up.

To make the caramel, use a heavy-bottomed pan and heat up the sugar and honey with the water until the liquid becomes clear. At this point, add the struffoli and the chopped angelica, and stir carefully until all the struffoli are coated with caramel. Arrange on a plate in the form of a crown. Decorate with silver balls (not too many) and leave to cool.

Le Bevande
wines and drinks

Non-alcoholic drinks

The most famous Italian mineral water is San Pellegrino, which comes from a source in a valley north of Bergamo. A small quantity of carbon dioxide is added to make it slightly sparkling. From another source, the same company produce Panna, which is a still mineral water, and also sold worldwide.

Some of the companies also market soft drinks such as water mixed with fruit juices. Aranciata San Pellegrino is the most popular, which is flavoured with orange. Limonata, in particular Chinotto (the forefather of Coca-Cola), is still very popular today. Aqua Brillante is based on ginger ale.

Aperitifs

The word 'aperitif' comes from the Latin 'aperire' (to open), and the aperitif is usually taken before a meal, to stimulate – or open – the appetite. The daily drinking of the Italians usually starts at about midday at the bar before lunch. It is not always alcoholic, as herb-flavoured, non-alcoholic drinks can be drunk instead.

But many aperitifs are based on alcohol, which can be drunk neat or diluted with water or soda water to make them more refreshing. One example is the herb-based Campari, which contains some 18 per cent alcohol, and tastes quite bitter. Another well-known Italian aperitif is Cynar, which is based on artichokes.

Many aperitifs are based on aromatic wines, which can be dry, sweet, white or red. They include Traminer, Verduzzo, Torlano and Prosecco, which are all drunk chilled. Vermouth is the best known wine-based aperitif, made with the addition of aromatic herbs. Martini and Cinzano are vermouths that have become popular the world over.

Wines

I was brought up in Monferrato, which is one of the best wine-producing areas in Italy. Later on I attended various courses to train as a sommelier and then spent many years dealing in wine. Over those years I heard some very fanciful descriptions of wines, and have since come to the very simple conclusion: a wine is good if you like it. Of course, with the help of a good guide you can develop a more refined palate. Price alone does not determine the quality of a wine; nor does the snobbery connected to labels.

Italy is the largest wine producer in the world. The Italian wine industry is not only producing vast quantities of wine, but – despite the sins of the past – wines of excellent quality, too. And the number of companies making exceptional wines that can be ranked with the finest wines in the world is growing. One such company, Antinori, celebrated 600 years of uninterrupted wine production in the late 1960s, early 1970s.

'Wine can be made from grapes, too,' says an old Italian proverb. To put a stop to any shady practices and to protect the consumer, in 1963 the Italian government brought in a new law. This forces the wine producer to declare the origin of its grapes and to meet very stringent requirements before receiving the 'Denominazione di Origine Controllata' (DOC), a mark of quality similar to France's 'Appellation Contrôlée'. There is a higher classification – 'Denominazione di Origine Controllata e Garantita' (DOCG) – which is awarded only to the very best wines. They include Barolo, Barbaresco, Chianti, Vino Nobile di Montepulciano and Brunello di Montalcino.

About 300 wines bear the DOC classification. The Chianti classification is the only one divided into two. Some bottles have a black cockerel ('Gallo Nero') label, and this marks the premier wine, Chianti Classico, grown in a small area between Florence and Siena. The  others, from six surrounding areas, carry a cherub ('Putto') label and are called after the locality.

Apart from DOC and DOCG wines, there are, of course, countless other local wines which are not generally known outside their own regions. Italians tend to drink the local wine. It would be hard to find a good Barolo in Sicily or a Nuragus di Sardegna in Lombardy, although that is changing a bit now. On the other hand, a vast range of Italian wines can be found abroad, and exports grow by 10 per cent every year.

Most of the wine consumed in Italy is everyday table wine. Although big wine drinkers, the Italians usually drink it only with meals, and sometimes as an aperitif.

Italians used to drink vast quantities of French champagne. But lately some Italian houses, particularly in the Veneto region and Conegliano, have been producing dry sparkling wines which are comparable to the French product.

Every region in Italy produces its own distinctive wines, be they red, white or rosé, and the characteristics depend on soil constitution, the position of the sun, the vintner's skill and the mixture of grapes used. The following is a broad outline of the major Italian wines, and an idea of which wine to drink with a particular type of dish. For an in-depth discussion of Italian wines, I suggest you read *Viva Vino 200: DOC and DOCG Wines and Wine Roads of Italy* (1985) by a friend of wine, Bruno Roncarati, who is one of the great connoisseurs of Italian wine.

Wine and food must be in harmony with each other. Generally speaking, the choice of wine depends on how the food is prepared, and how strong a flavour it has. It is pointless to serve a good wine with vinegar- or lemon-based dishes such as some antipasti or salads, or with citrus fruits. White wine goes well with seafood salad or cold antipasti; a rosé or light red wine (perhaps chilled) is good with hot antipasti. White meats such as chicken require a light wine, but if cooked with aromatic herbs and spices, then a wine of more robust nature is acceptable. Red meat, without a doubt, needs a full-bodied red wine; mature vintage wine is ideal for game dishes. The same rule applies for cheese. If the cheese is fresh and delicate, then a light wine is preferred; a stronger red one can be drunk with strong cheeses such as mature pecorino or Parmesan. Dessert wine is of prime importance too. Asti Spumante goes well with zabaglione and other light desserts, and Passito with cakes and fruit tarts.

Wines to accompany antipasti

As this is the first wine to be drunk at a meal, it should not be a heavy one. Many antipasti contain fish of some sort, and so need to be accompanied by a light, dry wine.

The best wines for seafood and oysters are the following: Pinot Grigio from Friuli and Trentino; Vermentino di Gallura from Sardinia; Muller Thurgau dell'Alto Adige; Cortese di Gavi and Erbaluce di Caluso from Piedmont; Blanc de Morgex from Val d'Aosta; Lugana della Lombardia; Orvieto from Umbria; Verdicchio di Jesi from the Marche; and Rapitala from Sicily.

For shellfish I would choose the following: Riesling Renano from the north, Corvo di Salaparuta Siciliano, Nuragus di Cagliari; Vernaccia di San Gimignano, Pinot Franciacorta from Lombardy; Greco di Tufo and Epomeo d'Ischia from Campania, and Soave del Veneto.

Various salami can be eaten with light red or rosé wines

which, of course, can be served chilled. I would suggest Rosato di Bolgheri from Tuscany, Kalterersee (a wine from Caldaro in Alto Adige) or Grignolino Piemontese.

Wines to accompany first courses

You might not think that there are good wines to accompany pasta or soup courses, but here are my suggestions. Obviously, if you have started a Pinot Grigio or Soave with the antipasto, then you can use the same along with a clear soup.

Wines for clear or vegetable soups might include a good quality Trebbiano di Romagna, a Tocai Lombardo or a Sylvaner del Trentino. In Piedmont, some country folk add a half glass of red table wine to soup. I've heard that the French in Périgord do the same. Buon appetito and santé!

For risotto or pasta with a fish sauce, I'd suggest a Grave del Friuli, Prosecco di Conegliano or a Gavi dei Gavi. In short, any good-quality wine, not forgetting Bianco di Custoza.

For risotto and pasta with a meat sauce, light red wines should be served: Sangiovese di Romagna, Dolcetto di Dogliani or Cabernet del Friuli. There are two wines from the Veneto region that are perfect along with the classic meat sauce – Valpolicella and Bardolino. Cannonau di Sardegna is excellent also. And if the sauce is cooked in the oven in the Sicilian style, then a Corvo Rosso should accompany it. My favourite wine for drinking with risotto with truffles is a young, slightly chilled Barbera d'Alba.

Wines to accompany fish

Fish is a very delicate food and is rarely cooked in highly spiced sauces, so accompany it with chilled dry white wine.

Falerno, which comes from the Campania region, is one of the great wines for fish. Excellent Tuscan varieties are Pomino di Frescobaldi and Bianco di Pitigliano. Also good are the Roman Est Est Est, Frascati and Marino, and the white wines of Friuli and Trentino such as Riesling Italico and Cabernet.

If the fish is more highly spiced and aromatic, as it might be when grilled, I would suggest an excellent rosé wine from Puglia called Five Roses, produced by Leone de Castris. It should be served very cold. Be careful though – it has a 13 per cent alcohol content!

Wines to accompany meat, poultry and game

Let's start with the white meats – veal and chicken. For those, we require a red wine with a full, but not heavy, flavour. Piedmont produces excellent wines: Fara Novarese, Sizzano, a young Carema, Ghemme and Donnaz. From Veneto come Merlot and Breganze.

For red meat we can go a step higher. Again from Piedmont, we have Nebbiolo, Carema Riserva, Boca and Barbera del Monferrato. Tuscany produces Nipozzano, Nobile di Montepulciano and Carmignano. Torgiano comes from Umbria, Rosso Piceno from Marche, and Aglianico del Vulture and Cannonau come from Sardinia.

Highly flavoured game dishes demand the highest quality of wine. Barolo and Barbaresco are de luxe wines, matured for four to five years at least.

Vino Nobile di Montepulciano, Brunello di Montalcino, Sassicaia, Tignanello and Solaia are the great wines of Tuscany. Grumello comes from the Valtellina and is a good-quality wine. In Naples, they drink Taurasi.

Wines to accompany cheese

Wines for soft, fermented cheeses should have a special character – not full bodied, but well balanced with not too high an alcoholic content. The ideal ones would be Santa Maddalena from the South Tyrol, or St Magdalener as they say in German. Going farther south, we find Pinot Nero dei Colli Orientali del Friuli, then on to the Val d'Aosta where we find Donnaz. In Piedmont there is the Grignolino and in Veneto the Bardolino. Both are excellent with cheese.

To serve with hard, matured cheeses, we find we need wines with a fuller-bodied quality, but not necessarily with a high alcoholic content. Carema, Nebbiolo, Spanna and most of all Barbera d'Asti are perfect accompaniments to Parmesan; while provolone and pecorino are best served with wines from the central southern parts of Italy, such as Chianti, Rosso di Cerignola or Cannonau di Sardegna.

Wines to accompany fruit

Because fruit has a high acid content, it does not go well with wine. For stewed fruit or cooked pears, I would suggest a Brachetto d'Acqui, a Freisa d'Asti from Piedmont or, naturally, a Lambrusco di Sorbara from Emilia.

Wines to accompany desserts

The most famous sparkling dessert wine is Asti Spumante. It is a wine for special occasions, and is consumed most at Christmas to accompany the famous panettone or other cakes. Another sparkling wine, but slightly dry, is the Prosecco di Valdobbiadene.

Fruit tarts and special sweets such as cannoli alla siciliana call for a sweeter, liqueur-type wine. Italy has many of them. The ones that I would recommend are: Torcolato, Picolit, Malvasia di Castelnuovo Don Bosco, Moscato Naturale d'Asti, Vin Santo di Gambellara and Sciacchetrà. It is traditional in Tuscany to dip cantucci, which are almond biscuits, into Vin Santo. Others are Aleatico di Gradoli, a sweet wine from Lazio; Aleatico di Puglia, Moscato di Trani, Primitivo di Manduria, Malvasia di Lipari, Moscato di Noto, the latter originating from the island of Pantelleria; Giro di Cagliari, Malvasia di Cagliari, Monica di Sardegna, Nasco di Cagliari, and Vernaccia di Oristano. And to go with chocolate, I would suggest a Barolo Chinato.

Digestifs

After the meal, dessert wines and coffee, comes the digestif, which is supposed to aid digestion, and usually consists of brandy, grappa or amaro. In Piedmont, they are generally known as 'pussacaffè' which translates as 'push down the coffee'. In the north of Italy, they add a little alcohol to their espresso, which then becomes 'corretto' (or corrected!).

In the arc of the Alps they use grappa for this purpose, the acqua vita of Italy. This is a spirit distilled from the grapes, skins and pips after the grapes have been pressed for wine. In Emilia Romagna they use a walnut liqueur, Nocino, which is made from macerated unripe walnuts. In the south it is more likely to be a liqueur based on aniseed such as Anisetta (which is ouzo like) or Sambuca, based on star anise seeds. (The coffee bean and the setting alight are optional…) In Sardinia they drink Filu Ferru, which is based on grappa.

The most pungent digestif is Fernet Branca, which is also good for stomach upsets (and hangovers)!

index

Note: Vegetarian dishes include eggs and dairy products, and are shown in **bold** type. Page numbers in **bold** denote major sections, those in *italic* illustrations.

A

Acciughe Ripiene al Forno 22
Acciughe in Salsa Verde 21, 23, *23*
Agnello al Forno con Patate 135
Agnolotti, Burro e Salvia 59
Alici in Tortiera 102, *103*
anchovies 16–17
    anchovy fillets in green sauce 21, 23, *23*
    baked anchovies (or sardines) with oregano 102, *103*
    baked stuffed anchovies 22
    garlic sauce with crudités 187
    savoy cabbage salad 186
    stuffed peppers and aubergines 153
    veal in tuna sauce 27
    yellow peppers with bagna cauda 36, *37*
Anguilla in Carpione 24
Animelle con Limone e Capperi 146, *147*
antipasti see starters
aperitifs 218
Arrosto di Maiale 138, *139*
artichokes
    artichokes the jewish way 158, *159*
    stewed artichokes 156
Asparagi alla Milanese 155
asparagus
    asparagus with fried eggs 155
    asparagus risotto 52
    cream of asparagus soup 45
aubergines
    baked aubergine with cheese and tomato 154
    sautéed aubergines 178
    stuffed peppers and aubergines 153

B

Baccalà in Umido 110
Bagna Cauda 187
basil 14–15

beans
    curly endive and cannellini beans 165
    french bean salad with mint 185
    french beans with tomato *113*, 150
    pasta with beans 65
beef 9, 96–8
    beef steak with pizzaiola sauce 122
    beef stock 40
    boiled mixed meats from piedmont 124–5
    braised beef with red wine 126, *127*
    cold fillet of beef with green sauce 121
    gourmet lasagne 78–9, *79*
    meat loaf in tomato sauce 123
    pappardelle with roast beef sauce 64
Bietole al Burro 167
Biscotti di Meliga 207, 214
Bollito Misto alla Piemontese 124–5
Brasato al Nebbiolo 126, *127*
bread 13
    bread and tomato salad 182
    breadsticks 93
    home-style bread 94, *95*
    pizza bread with rosemary 92
Brodo di Carne 40
Brodo di Gallina 40
Brodo di Pesce 41
Bucatini alla Carbonara 74
Busie d'la Nonna 213

C

cabbage, savoy cabbage salad 186
Calamari Fritti 106
Calzoncini Fritti 90
Calzone Imbottito 88, *89*
Camoscio in Salmí 120
Cannoli alla Siciliana 211
Cappellacci al Sugo di Porcini 60, *61*
Cappelle di Porcini alla Griglia 164
Carciofi alla Giudea 158, *159*
Carciofi in Umido 156
Carote Fritte 169
carrots, **fried carrots** 169

celery, **tomato and celery salad** 184
ceps *see* mushrooms
cereals and grains 12–13
chard, **swiss chard with butter** 167
cheeses 17, **190–99**
    baked aubergine with cheese and tomato 154
    deep-fried mozzarella 198
    easter cake 160
    fondue with truffle 197
    fresh 196
    fried smoked mozzarella 199, *199*
    hard 192–3
    pick-me-up (*tiramisú*) 209
    ricotta tart 210
    semi-soft 194
    soft 195
    tomato and cheese pizza 87
    wines to accompany 221
chickens 9–10, 96
    see also poultry
    boiled mixed meats from piedmont 124–5
    chicken escalopes with capers and lemon 112, *113*
    chicken stock 40
    roast chicken with potatoes 111
    stuffed chicken legs 114
chicory, dressed chicory 172, *173*
Cicoria e Fagioli 165
Cicoria Vestita 172, *173*
Cime di Rapa Aglio e Olio 170
Cocozielli e Ova 161
cod *see* fish and seafood
Coniglio Arrosto con Patate 118, *119*
Coniglio San Angelo 117
Coscia di Pollo Ripiena 114
Coscia Marinata alla Griglia 136
Costine di Maiale con Ceci 140
Cotoletta alla Milanese 129
courgettes
    courgette and egg 161
    fried courgette salad 35
    stuffed courgette flowers 30, *31*
Cozze al Forno 25
Crema di Funghi Porcini 44
Crostata di Lamponi 205

D

desserts *see* fruit and desserts
digestifs 221
drinks and wines **218–21**

E

eel, marinated eel 24
equipment 18, *18–19*

F

Fagiolini alla Napoletana *113*, 150
Fegato alla Veneziana 143
Fegato Burro e Salvia 142, *147*
fennel, **baked fennel** 149, 171, *171*
Festoni del Ghiottone 78–9, *79*
Fettuccine Nere con Peoci 76, *77*
Filetto Freddo con Salsa Verde 121
Finocchi Gratinati 149, 171, *171*
Fiori di Zucchini Ripieni 30, *31*
first course **38–95**
    wines to accompany 220
fish and seafood 10, 96
    anchovies *see* anchovies
    baked mussels 25
    black fettuccine with mussels, garlic and parsley 76, *77*
    black risotto 48
    fish soup *42*, 43
    fish stock 41
    fried squid 106
    grilled swordfish 'muddica' 99
    little puglian ears with seafood and cherry tomatoes 72, *73*
    marinated eel 24
    mixed fried fish 100, *101*
    prawn ravioli 63
    prawns in garlic, oil and chilli sauce 107
    salt cod salad 108, *109*
    salt cod in tomatoes 110
    seafood salad 26
    seafood spaghettini 68
    turbot with a piquant sauce 104, *105*
    wines to accompany 220
flour 12
Focaccia al Rosmarino 92
Fonduta con Tartufi 197
Fragole all'Aceto Balsamico con Pepe 202